Secrets of the Manatee

Secrets of the Manatee

An Insider's Guide to Florida's Most Iconic Marine Mammal

Diane Morgan

PINEAPPLE PRESS
Palm Beach, Florida

Pineapple Press
An imprint of Globe Pequot, the trade division of
The Rowman & Littlefield Publishing Group, Inc.
4501 Forbes Blvd., Ste. 200
Lanham, MD 20706
www.rowman.com

Distributed by NATIONAL BOOK NETWORK

British Library Cataloguing in Publication Information available

Library of Congress Cataloging-in-Publication Data

Names: Morgan, Diane, 1947- author.
Title: Secrets of the manatee : an insider's guide to Florida's most iconic marine mammal / Diane Morgan.
Description: Palm Beach Florida : Pineapple Press, [2023] | Includes index.
Identifiers: LCCN 2022038825 (print) | LCCN 2022038826 (ebook) | ISBN 9781683343486 (paperback) | ISBN 9781683343493 (epub)
Subjects: LCSH: West Indian manatee—Florida.
Classification: LCC QL737.S63 M67 2023 (print) | LCC QL737.S63 (ebook) | DDC 599.5509759—dc23/eng/20220817
LC record available at https://lccn.loc.gov/2022038825
LC ebook record available at https://lccn.loc.gov/2022038826

∞™ The paper used in this publication meets the minimum requirements of American National Standard for Information Sciences—Permanence of Paper for Printed Library Materials, ANSI/NISO Z39.48-1992.

To the Manatees.

I waded into the river
and suddenly a door
in the water opened inward . . .

—Elizabeth Bishop, "The Riverman"

Contents

Acknowledgments

I would like to thank everyone who helped make this book a reality by generously sharing with me, in one way or another, their time, knowledge, and expertise. I appreciate the heroic efforts you've made, the knowledge you've gained and shared, and the love you radiate for our sea cow friends.

Some of y'all just made me laugh.

To the team at Pineapple Press: Acquisitions Editor Lauren Younker, her able and super-excellent assistant Deb Murphy, Meaghan Menzel, and everyone—you've made my life so much easier!

Very, very special thanks to Dr. Beth Brady of Mote Marine Laboratory who helped me in more ways than she knows. Her generosity in letting me get a close look at her research into manatee communication was thrilling!

Thanks to Harbor Branch Oceanographic Institute for allowing me to participate in The Manatee Project (among other things). Sitting around observing and counting manatees is the best volunteer job anyone could ever have.

The Save the Manatee Club, Florida Fish and Wildlife, Defenders of Wildlife, Mote Marine Laboratory and Aquarium, The Manatee Observation and Education Center (including the snake Diego), Zoo Tampa, Sirenian International, and the Manatee Rescue & Rehabilitation Partnership. All doing supremely important work for our sirenian friends.

Craig Pittman, brilliant author of many brilliant books (including the inimitable *Manatee Insanity*), podcaster, intrepid environmental reporter and all-around nice person.

Dr. Dennis Hanisak, whose unrelenting efforts to save seagrass may also save the day! You're a star in my book.

Dr. Jim Masterson, knower of all things, teacher, friend, and genuinely great guy.

Steve Burton, Director of FAU's Stranding and Population Assessment and the kindest person.

And, as always, love to my husband John Warner and our bloodhounds, Charlotte and Elmer.

And in memory of Ricky, who was there for me always.

Official Manatee Classification

INTEGRATED TAXONOMIC INFORMATION SYSTEM

Kingdom Animalia: This group includes all animals, from microscopic parasites related to jellyfish to gigantic blue whales.

Subkingdom Bilateria: Animals in this group have bilateral symmetry, nice and even. Animals like sponges, jellies, and sea stars don't have this feature.

Infrakingdom Deuterostomia: In this bilateral group, the development of the anus begins before the formation of the mouth during embryonic development. For some reason this is a very important distinction.

Phylum Chordata: In some stage of their development, members of this group, which includes all vertebrates as well as lancelets and tunicates, have a notochord, dorsally situated central nervous system, and gill slit.

Subphylum Vertebrata: Animals in this group typically have a bony or cartilaginous spinal column, a distinct head and brain, and an internal skeleton.

Infraphylum Gnathostomata: Vertebrates in this group have upper and lower jaws.

Superclass Tetrapoda: Animals in this group have two pairs of limbs—in manatees one pair is vestigial but still there.

Class Mammalia: Mammals in this group nourish their young with milk secreted by mammary glands.

Subclass Theria: In this group, members give birth to live young without using a shelled egg. It's still a large group, since it includes all mammals except monotremes (platypuses and echidnas).

Infraclass Eutheria: These are the true placentals. It includes all mammals except monotremes and marsupials like kangaroos.

Order Sirenia: It is only at this point in the evolutionary tree that manatees diverge from humans. Members of this group are all large marine herbivores. The only members are manatees and dugongs. Other mammals shuffled off somewhere else.

Family Trichechidae: This is the point at which manatees and dugongs split. Manatees are larger, with different kinds of teeth, tail, snout, and geographic distribution. Several extinct manatee species are included in this group.

Genus *Trichechus*: This group comprises all three species of extant manatees, listed below.

Species

- *Trichechus inunguis* (Amazonian manatee)
- *Trichechus senegalensis* (African manatee)
- *Trichechus manatus* (West Indian manatee)

Subspecies

- *Trichechus manatus manatus* (Antillean manatee)
- *Trichechus manatus latirostris* (Florida manatee)

Top FAQs

1. *Are manatees mammals?* Yes. They breathe air, give birth to live young, and even have hair. Sort of.
2. *What is the plural of manatee?* Manatee. Or manatees. It really does not matter. "Sea cows" is fine, too.
3. *How much do they weigh?* On the average, about half a ton. A big one (usually a female) however, can top three thousand pounds.
4. *How big are manatees when they are born?* About sixty pounds.
5. *What do they eat?* Primarily sea grass and other vegetation.
6. *What is the gestation period?* About thirteen months.
7. *Do manatees live in family groups?* No, just mother and calf. But large numbers can gather for social activity or to feed together.
8. *Are manatees aggressive?* No, they are harmless to humans and other animals.
9. *How fast can manatees swim?* Generally, about five miles an hour, but they can crank up to twenty miles an hour for brief periods.
10. *How often do manatees need to breathe?* Every five minutes when active, every twenty when resting.
11. *Do manatees make noise?* Yes, they can squeal and squeak under water.
12. *Are manatees going extinct?* One hopes not, but these are perilous times. Every time we seem to be making some progress in saving them, some natural disaster or politically boneheaded move sets everything back again.
13. *How many manatees are there in Florida?* Probably about ten thousand.
14. *Are manatees closely related to dolphins?* No. They are related to dugongs and, surprisingly, elephants, aardvarks, and hyraxes.
15. *Are manatees native to Florida?* Yes. They have been here for thousands of years.
16. *How long do they live?* The oldest known manatee was healthy at age sixty-nine and died by accident.
17. *Can manatees live in cold water?* No, manatees can die if the water temperature drops below 68 degrees Fahrenheit (20 degrees Celsius) for a period of time.

Introduction

Chris Columbus Meets the Mermaids

It is January 8, 1493. Christopher Columbus, having already stumbled into the New World, is about to make an even more momentous discovery. Sailing near what is now the Dominican Republic, he notes carefully in his log: "Saw three mermaids." Then he adds with a sniff, "They are not half so beautiful as they have been painted," after getting a good look at their faces. They were humanlike "only after a fashion," he complained, then going on to grumble about their "masculine features." This is the first recorded mention of manatees by a European.

Apparently, Columbus had a knack for spotting manatees (or "mermaids"). He claimed he had seen some earlier, off the coast of Guinea during one of his early African voyages. He was probably telling the truth, since manatees do indeed inhabit the coasts of both the Dominican Republic in the New World and Guinea in the Old. However, the West African variety is a separate species, thus making Columbus the first person on record to note the existence of both kinds. For some reason, Columbus hasn't been given sufficient credit for this. His high marks for failing geography and destroying native cultures takes precedence.

Later, in 1494, Columbus mentioned seeing "swarms" of them at the freshwater springs in the Bahia de Cochinos region of Cuba. They are still found there.

Columbus wasn't the only early explorer to mention manatees. The Portuguese writer António

During Roman times, the classical poet Ovid had a word to say about sea cows. Writing about the great flood, he tosses in this line: "Ugly sea-cows float where slender she-goats used to nibble." Since Ovid could know nothing about manatees and probably not much about dugongs, your guess is as good as any regarding what he was talking about. Possibly mermaids. To be fair, the word Ovid used was "phoca," which can apply to any marine mammal. So I think the translator, Rolfe Humphries, was being a bit unfair not only to Ovid, which is forgivable, but also to manatees, which is not.

It is true that manatees remind many people of cows, hence their other name: sea cow. Even in German the word for manatee is *Seekuh*, or sea cow, although its look-alike cousin the dugong is called *Seeschwein*, or "sea pig." Germans also know the guinea pig as *Meersweinchen*, or "little ocean pig," for reasons beyond the scope of this book. More sensibly, the porcupine is called *Stachelschwein*, or "spike pig." Pigs seem to be an important part of German culture.

Galvão proclaimed in 1497 there dwelled a "fish called manatim; is big and has a cow's head and face, and also in the flesh it looks very like it . . . and the female has breasts with nipples that feeds its children who are born alive."

The earliest depiction of the West Indian manatee was created about 1535 and included in the book *La Historia de la Indias* by Gonzalo Fernandez de Oviedo y Valdez (1478–1557), who is also the first person to register the name "manatee" in Castilian Spanish (1526). It's not a very good likeness, although it does accurately portray the torpedo-shaped body and was widely copied. He wrote, "The manatee is a fish of the sea, a big one, and is far larger than a shark in greatness and length and is very ugly." As an aside, Oviedo is also the first person known to have discussed hammocks, pineapples, and tobacco.

Nearly one hundred years later, in 1590, the Spanish Jesuit naturalist Diaz Acosta Facundo announced, "In the islands of Barlavento, namely Spanish Cuba, Puerto Rico, Jamaica, there is the so-called manatee, a strange kind of fish, if one can name fish to an animal, whose cubs are born alive, and has teats, and with milk, they are raised and eat herbs in the fields; but indeed, usually resides in the water." He went on to mention that because it was a "fish," manatees could be eaten on Fridays, though he felt kind of bad about it. He wrote, "When I ate it on a Friday, I almost had scruples, because its color and flavoring seemed like nothing but veal chops or knuckle chops."

Another drawing, done slightly later (1605), is by pioneering botanist Carolus Clusius. Clusius should have stuck to drawing tulips, a plant that fascinated him. The original is housed in the Library of the Madrid Botanical Gardens. Clusius was born in France, died in the Netherlands, and considered himself Belgian, so there was a lot of confusion right from the start. Clusius's manatee has a squarish tail, large, mournful eyes, and very handlike flippers.

In 1647 Father Cristavao de Lisboa drew a manatee both from the side and bottom. This attempt shows a manatee with long, sprouting whiskers and awkwardly bent flippers with what appear to be claws rather than fingernails at the end. The underside view shows female genitalia and very pronounced breasts under the flippers.

Over the years manatees have continued to fascinate those of us who are fortunate enough to meet them. They share their strange appeal with other natural oddities like sloths, pandas, naked mole-rats, meerkats, koalas, and octopuses (you can go right ahead and say "octopi" if you want, or if you're a purist, octopodes. Don't let anyone stop you. You have your rights).

Diving Deeper

Manatees and Their In-Laws (Not Whales)

Manatees are in a class by themselves. Beneath their gray pebbled hide, between their whiskery snouts and their paddle tail, is a mystery. The manatee has attributes unlike any other animal on earth (or in the ocean). Its metabolism is as slow as a sloth's, but it can swim as fast as dolphin, at least briefly. It can weigh a ton and a half, yet it glides through the water with the silent grace of an eel. It produces teeth in a conveyer-like way, seemingly unendingly. It can live in both fresh and brackish water. Manatees are untroubled by sharks and gators. They even tolerate human presence, when we invade their waters to "swim with the manatees." They get along swimmingly with their own kind but are perfectly self-sufficient, enjoying but not needing any better company than themselves. They are famously small brained, and yet science has shown that they can learn anything a dolphin can. (Brain size doesn't correlate with intelligence as well as one might think.) They possess uncanny wisdom.

People used to think that manatees were some sort of subtropical walrus, a forgivable error, despite the fact that the two marine mammals have little in common other than a large gray body and slightly wistful expression. In anatomy, physiology, distribution, evolutionary history, behavior, and diet (clams casino vs. the salad bar), they couldn't be more different. (Some sources claim they are "completely unrelated." Not true. All animals are related. It's just a question of how closely.)

At one time, these peaceful, long-lived mammals had an idyllic life. With no predators to bother them and no prey to bother themselves with, they could spend their days moseying from one rich underwater meadow to the next, gathering with friends, raising their calves, and working on their stamp collections. Then humans showed up.

Since our arrival to Florida (around seven thousand years or so ago), manatees have had a rough deal. These hapless creatures have been hunted by humans, hit by boats, gouged by propellers, and ridden by tourists as well as had their homes fouled by pollution. Less popular than their flashier fellow marine mammal, the dolphin, they have been under-researched and underappreciated. Many more scientists have devoted their careers to studying dolphins, whales, and even sharks.

An algae-encrusted manatee surrounded by fish. Everyone benefits: the manatee provides habitat for the algae; the algae protect the manatee from the sun; the fish eat the algae to prevent overgrowth; the manatee provides shade and protection for the fish. Source: *Keith Ramos, USFWS ROYALTY FREE (PIXNIO-29372-3000x2008)*

This lack of appreciation is exemplified by the nineteenth-century American author Herman Melville (1819–1891). In his very long, ghastly novel *Moby-Dick*, he wrote:

> I am aware that down to the present time, the fish styled Lamatins [manatees] and Dugongs (Pig-fish and Sow-fish of the Coffins of Nantucket) are included by many naturalists among the whales. But as these pigfish are a nosy, contemptible set, mostly lurking in the mouths of rivers, and feeding on wet hay, and especially as they do not spout, I deny their credentials as whales; and have presented them with their passports to quit the Kingdom of Cetology.

Melville was not only dismissive of manatees, but he was also wrong about whales. He thought they were fish.

Let's get that straight right away. Manatees are mammals. They breathe air, give birth to live young, have warm blood, and even sport whiskers.

Manatees are not just mammals; they are *big* mammals. (The Florida manatee is the largest marine herbivore on earth.) Some of them are *really* big. A run-of-the-mill manatee weighs in at half a ton; a really huge one can top three thousand pounds. Indeed, all marine mammals attain a decent size, and some of them, like whales, are really huge. Manatees' massive size is their only real defense; they have no tusks, sharp teeth, or hooves.

The Florida manatee's official name is *Trichechus manatus latirostris*, which is admittedly quite a mouthful. It belongs to the order Sirenia (after the sirens of legend), the

Disturbingly, large mammals have steadily shrunk in numbers or gone extinct altogether since the dawn of human hunting. Giant sloths, mammoths, and mastodons have all disappeared since the arrival of predatory humans, although we should note that our best friend, the dog, helped in the extirpation process.

genus *Trichechus* ("whiskery"), the species *manatus* (meaning "with hands" or possibly "breasts"), and the subspecies *latirostris* (broad snouted). Thus, the Florida manatee is a bewhiskered, behanded, wide-snouted thingamabob. The common name *manatee* seems to derive from the Carib word *manati*, meaning breast or udder. The ancient Taino people who named them recognized quite clearly that they weren't dealing with fish. Perhaps the Europeans didn't like or understand that term and chose to use the similar-sounding, equally accurate, but unrelated Latin *manatus*, meaning hand.

It and its close kin, the Antillean manatee (*T. manatus manatus*) are subspecies of the West Indian manatee (*Trichechus manatus*). This division of the species into two subcategories was first proposed in 1934 but not confirmed until the 1980s, using slight differences in the structure of the skull. It's very difficult to tell them apart by just looking, even for experts. Antillean manatees tend to run a bit smaller, much lighter, and somewhat less round, although both species are sort of spindle shaped. (Scientists like the word "fusiform.") The major factor separating the subspecies is geographical—the deep water and strong currents in the Straits of Florida. The Florida and Antillean manatee generally occupy different areas. They can probably interbreed, if tempted, but they just don't often encounter each other.

All manatees are members of the order Sirenia, which brings us back to Columbus and his mermaids. However, in mythology, sirens and mermaids are not the same. The first recorded "mermaid" was the fourth century BCE Babylonian god Oannes (half fish/half human) who would leave the sea every day only to return at night.

In Greek myth, a siren was half woman and half bird, complete with a dulcet singing voice and wings. Mermaids, on the other hand, are half women and half fish. Mermaids spend most of their time combing their hair and looking in mirrors. Originally, it seems, nothing is mentioned about their singing abilities, although that soon changed. In T. S. Eliot's "The Love Song of J. Alfred Prufrock," the speaker claims to have heard mermaids singing "each to each."

There are also mermen who have developed an unpleasant reputation in Scottish and Irish folklore. They are said to possess small, piggy eyes and breath that stinks of rotten fish. Their noses are flushed from consuming too much brandy from the ships they wrecked. I suppose I should have mentioned the shipwrecking part first.

In contrast, Scandinavian mermen are good-looking chaps, usually with green beards and hair. They live peacefully at the bottom of the sea and harm no one.

Shakespeare himself mentioned mermaids, although whether the Bard was a member of the "Fraternity of Sireniacal Gentlemen," which met the first Friday of every month for drinks at the Mermaid Tavern in Cheapside, is a matter of unresolvable dispute. Certainly Ben Jonson, John Donne, and other literary lights belonged. Alas, the tavern was destroyed in the Great Fire of London in 1666. In his plays, most of the Bard's references to mermaids were positive:

> Once I sat upon a promontory,
> And heard a mermaid on a dolphin's back
> Uttering such dulcet and harmonious breath
> That the rude sea grew civil at her song,
> And certain stars shot madly from their spheres,
> To hear the sea-maid's music?
> (William Shakespeare, *A Midsummer Night's Dream*)

However, he also pays homage to the darker side of the mermaid legend in Richard's soliloquy in part 3 of *Henry VI*: "I'll drown more sailors than the mermaid shall."

As a rule, mermaids have a nicer reputation than sirens, although the mermaids in J. M. Barrie's *Peter Pan* were nasty and vain. In one movie version, they also had very sharp, fanglike teeth, which is not manatee-like at all. Real manatees have only molars.

This is as good a place as any to mention Melusina, a freshwater mermaid of northern European folklore whose name means "melodious." Like the more classical mermaids, she has a woman's body and a fish tail (or, in some iterations, two tails!) She will take a human male for a lover so long as he promises to leave her alone while she bathes. Of course, he always breaks his oath, and she sweeps him into the water with her fishy tail (or tails) and drowns him. This tale has a sad ring nowadays, for humans have surely broken more than one oath to manatees. The manatees have yet to take adequate retaliation. The worst thing they can do to us is to disappear entirely and forever.

In any case, over the centuries, these two legendary creatures—sirens and mermaids—were conflated, which partially explains why manatees were shoved into a whimsically named genus, Sirenia, even though there is absolutely nothing birdlike or even songlike about them, except for a series of squeaks and chirps. It is an interesting sound, although hardly mesmerizing. Especially since you have to be underwater to hear it.

Today four species of Sirenia, separated into two families, inhabit the earth: three manatee species (Trichechidae family) and their close cousin, the dugong (*Dugong dugon*), which lives in the Indian and Pacific Oceans. The dugong has tragically been declared extinct in Chinese waters in 2022.

Sirenians have no close relations among walruses, dolphins, whales, or hippopotamuses. Their closest living terrestrial relatives are elephants, and they are kissing cousins to aardvarks and the east African rock hyrax, a peculiar, furry creature with mouselike ears, glaring eyes, sharp teeth, and a distinctly unpleasant expression that bears no resemblance to manatees in any way at all. Still, evolutionary biologists are quite firm on this point.

Manatees are "subungulates" (which means hoofed but with separate digits, even though manatees don't have hoofs and their digits are encased in their flippers) and, like all subungulates, belong to a "superorder," or clade, of mammals called Afrotheria—beasts of the African-Asian landmass. Afrotheria is one of four major groups in the Eutheria, or placental mammals.

Besides manatees, Afrotheria includes tenrecs, hyraxes, golden moles, sengis, aardvarks, elephants, and elephant shrews. In case you're wondering, elephant shrews are more closely related to aardvarks than to elephants or to shrews. (Don't worry if you have not heard of half of these critters. You're in good company.) None of them looks much like the others, and indeed, the common ancestry of these animals was not recognized until the late 1990s, when molecular and genetic studies uncovered the truth. The most notable anatomical point of resemblance among the members of this clade appears to be a long, mobile snout. Hyraxes, elephants, and manatees share another strange feature: a non-heart-shaped heart. Most of us mammals have hearts that come to a point at the bottom. Manatees and their kin have flat-bottomed hearts.

Although sirenians may be sparse nowadays, there were once dozens of species, most of them in the western Atlantic Ocean and Caribbean areas. Chief among them, however, living in the Pacific, was the gigantic Steller's sea cow (*Hydrodamalis gigas*), which was more than thirty feet long. These massive animals inhabited the icy waters off Alaska. I wish we had a good picture of them, but Georg Steller's expedition was too cheap to fund an artist, so poor Georg was forced to try to describe them. Steller managed to get about a dozen other Alaskan species named after himself, including the sea otter, a sea lion, the gumboot chiton, and my own favorite, the hoary mugwort (*Artemisia stelleriana*). He even managed to snag a mineral—stellerite. In any case, the giant sea cows were killed off by Russian sailors, fur traders, and seal hunters for their meat and fat in the eighteenth century, only about twenty-seven years after they were discovered. The Russians rightly get blamed for this catastrophe, although some researchers believe the Steller's sea cow was already on the brink of extinction when it was discovered. The Europeans just finished the job. In any case, the loss of this massive, toothless, benevolent creature is too painful to think about.

If you are a New Agey type (and really, who isn't?), manatees possess a wealth of otherworldly attributes invaluable in guiding us through life. According to the undoubtedly authoritative Whatismyspiritual animal.com, manatees as spiritual advisers suggest we slow down, take time to breathe, simplify our lives, and eat our vegetables. However, it warns bleakly, there is "someone" who doesn't have your best interest in mind. Be wary. If a manatee is your totem animal, however, it means you are a cuddler with little tolerance for violence. Many people will try to take advantage of your sweet disposition. You also have trouble making friends, because your intense energy can be frightening until people see how kind and gentle you are. That's when they start to take advantage of you, apparently. You should invoke manatee when you need to make slow and steady progress, but also to help you accept the inevitable, whatever that is. You should call upon manatee as a "power animal" when you need to trust yourself more. Spiritual manatees are also helpful in shapeshifting, although in real life they have only one shape: torpedo.

The dugongs are considered to be the family of greater antiquity. Ancient dugongs are also said to have been more "cosmopolitan," referring in this case not to their degree of sophistication, but to their widespread distribution compared to manatees. However, during the Pliocene age, their diversity decreased, and ultimately manatees won the evolutionary

Clade studies have revolutionized biology. They have revealed, for example, that fungi are more closely related to animals than they are to plants. Vegans may thus soon have to swear off mushrooms, and that would be a shame.

struggle and replaced dugongs in places where they once cohabited (and I mean that in the nicest possible way). Nowhere in today's world do manatees and dugongs inhabit the same ecosystem. In fact, they are oceans apart. But once they lived cheek by jowl.

Manatees, on the other hand, despite all belonging to one genus, are divided into three species: the Amazonian manatee (*T. manatus inunguis*), the West African manatee (*T. manatus senegalensis*), and two subspecies of West Indian manatee (*T. manatus manatus* and *T. manatus latirostris*). The last is our Florida manatee.

The Amazonian manatee gets its scientific name "*inunguis*" from the fact that, unlike its congeneric friends, it has no fingernails. True to its common name, it lives in the Amazon River basin. It's a freshwater species and quite a bit smaller than the others. The West Indian manatee can be found in the southeastern United States (the Florida manatee) and discontinuously throughout the Caribbean, all the way down to the northwestern coast of Brazil.

The West African manatee is found off the coast of Africa. Scientists believe, after churning through incredibly complex and messy fossil and genetic records, that manatees originated in South America and gradually reached the west coast of Africa at a time when the Atlantic was a lot narrower and shallower than it is now. Researchers Erica Martinha Silva de Souza and her colleagues reached this conclusion after sequencing the complete mitogenomes of all living species of manatees to discover their phylogenetic relationships and to figure out when the species began to diverge and how natural selection worked on mitochondrial genes (which have their own, very special DNA) during manatee evolution.

The split among manatee species apparently occurred during the Pleistocene, about 1.34 million years ago. Scientists learned that the West Indian and West African manatee were more closely related to each other than to the Amazonian manatee, a discovery that is not really surprising. Even to a casual onlooker like myself, the fingernails alone give it away.

At one time or another there were about thirty-five distinct species of sirenians, each munching on a slightly different kind of herbage. Gradually, most of them fell to the axe of extinction, leaving today only the dugongs of the Indian and Pacific Oceans and the manatees of the New World and West Africa. All are called sea cows. It is not completely understood why so many earlier species have disappeared, although it has been suggested that the changing quality or quantity of seagrass contributed to the culling process. Manatees, unlike dugongs, developed specialized "marching molars" that allowed them

Presumably manatee fingernails are reminders of the days long gone when manatees lived on land. I don't know why Amazonian manatees gave up on them completely.

to consume seagrasses that were getting tougher and more fibrous by the year. Dugongs were just unable to compete. Today the single living species of dugongs (*Dugong dugon*) is found only in the Indian and western Pacific Oceans. It's hard to think of manatees as outcompeting anyone, but the fossil record does not lie.

SEA COWS IN PROGRESS: THE EVOLUTION OF MANATEES

Unraveling the evolutionary mess that cooked up the manatee (and its cousin the dugong) is not a task for the fainthearted. It is a trail winding through fifty or sixty million years, with many cross paths and dead ends. Ancestors such as the Prorastomus, Protosiren, Potamosiren, and Ribodon all played a part. The earliest ancestors were four-legged wading creatures that inhabited rivers and shallow estuaries. We have fossil examples from both the Caribbean and Mediterranean areas. The oldest known sirenian is Prorastomus, from early Eocene Jamaica. Just as they do today, ancient sirenians inhabited rivers, lagoons, estuaries, and nearshore marine waters.

Another early (and better preserved) example is *Pezosiren portelli*. The "type specimen" (specimen selected to serve as a reference point) of Pezosiren is a Jamaican fossil skeleton, described in 2001 by Daryl Domning, a marine mammal paleontologist at Howard University in Washington, DC, and one of the world's leading experts on Sirenia. "Pezo" means walking, "siren" of course refers to siren/mermaids, and "portelli" honors Roger W. Portell, who unearthed the site. Dr. Portell is currently the collection director of Invertebrate Paleontology and Micropaleontology at the Florida Museum of Natural History.

Pezosiren looked like a cross between a pig and a hippo and had a powerful tail. Pezosiren were about two yards long. Like modern manatees, it was a vegetarian and lived about fifty million years ago. It is considered a "transitional species," reverting from land back to water. Pezosiren probably had a lifestyle similar to that of a modern hippopotamus. We know it had four legs perfectly adapted to walking, rather than flippers, but possessed a very manatee-like skull and tooth structure. It also had marine-specialized features, like retracted nostrils. That and the presence of heavy, ballast-like ribs shows that it spent most of its time in the water.

Over time, the pelvic bones grew small and detached from the backbone. The hindlimbs, of course, have completely disappeared. (The manatees' five fingerbones, left over from the time when manatees were terrestrial, are still apparent but are encased within the flipper.) David Kingsley from Stanford University started weighing manatee pelvic bones. In almost every case, the left pelvic bone outweighed the right one by about 10 percent. This struck an interesting note. The same phenomenon has been seen in three species of stickleback fish, who, in the course of their own evolutionary journey, needed to develop a more streamlined profile. In the case of the sticklebacks, rescue came in the form of a PitX1 gene mutation, a mutation that also results in hind-legless mice. In both those cases, the left pelvic bone was the larger one. Kingsley thinks the same mutation may be at work here but still lacks the evidence to prove it. At the time of this writing, he's looking at other legless species to see if the same phenomenon holds. Apparently, he is in need of a good supply of snake and whale pelvises.

By the end of the Eocene, the dugong family had appeared—sirenians with fully aquatic, streamlined bodies, flippers, no hind limbs, and powerful tails.

Our "modern" manatee family, the Trichechidae, came last. They apparently arose from early dugongids in the late Eocene or early Oligocene, 6.56 million years ago. With the exception of Steller's sea cow, all remained tropical.

As the seagrasses continued to flourish and diversify, sirenians of all sorts did the same, achieving reaching peak diversity during the Miocene, exactly when the seagrasses were also at their height. So, for millions upon millions of years, the fate of manatees has been linked to that of the grasses they depend upon.

Where Manatees Live

Home Sweet Home

True to its name, today the Florida manatee is pretty much restricted to peninsular Florida for year-round living, although that may change as the climate heats up. Although Florida manatees are identical to each other both genetically and anatomically, scientists have identified four regional groups or subpopulations (also called "management units"), depending on their preferred Florida refuges: Atlantic, Upper St. Johns, Northwest, and Southwest. East Coast manatees live between Miami in the south and the St. John's River to the north. On the Gulf Coast, there's a good population in Everglades National Park all the way up to the Suwanee River. They are less common in the Keys. Interestingly, manatees move up and down the coasts, occasionally straying into an area adjacent to their own population headquarters; however, they rarely move from coast to coast.

When they are hanging around in the ocean, manatees naturally produce ADH (antidiuretic hormone), which helps them conserve their own body water. After a week or so in the ocean, even the versatile Florida manatee gets thirsty and must drink fresh water.

When in fresh water, they switch over to producing aldosterone, a steroid hormone secreted by the adrenal glands that helps them retain sodium. Being a manatee is trickier than it may appear at first glance. We do know that manatees can inhabit fresh water forever, but their tolerance for a complete saltwater environment is not fully understood. At one time it was believed that manatees did not need fresh water (a hypothesis based on urine data, renal anatomy, and the fact that people saw them in salt water a lot). Although manatees were observed drinking fresh water from hoses and other fresh water sources, some scientists thought they might be just "playing."

To get to the bottom of things, scientists at the Physiological Ecology and Bioenergetics Lab (PEBL) at the University of Central Florida worked with some captive West Indian manatees in Florida (a lot of paperwork required) and Brazil (possibly less paperwork, possibly more). They also got some blood from some free-ranging manatees in Puerto Rico and Colombia.

A diver passively observes a surfacing manatee. Getting too close to a wild manatee can be considered harassment, which is defined as actions that alter a manatee's natural behavior. Although Florida manatees are considered marine mammals, they are perfectly happy in fresh or brackish water as well. The fancy word for this kind of adaptation is "euryhaline," and few animals are able to swim freely between these extremes. Amazonian manatees, for instance, are restricted to fresh water, whereas dugongs can tolerate only salt water. But Florida manatees possess kidneys specialized to osmoregulate their internal water and salt balance. Source: Keith Ramos, USFWS ROYALTY FREE (PIXNIO-29334-3000x2008)

The idea was to see how manatees handled several experimental conditions: animals living in fresh water eating lettuce (94 percent water content); animals living in salt water eating lettuce; and animals living in salt water eating seagrasses (high in salt content and low in water content), both with and without access to fresh water to drink. In each case the scientists measured how much fresh water they drank and how much they obtained directly from the food they were eating (using labeled water dilution) and their ability to maintain electrolyte and water balance.

It turned out that within nine days, captive manatees in salt water that were fed seagrass without access to fresh water developed major increases in plasma concentrations of sodium and chloride. Eventually, the manatees just stopped eating seagrass. This indicates that wild manatees need regular access to fresh, or at least brackish, water.

Since we now know that manatees absolutely need fresh water to survive, perhaps their designation as a marine mammal is a bit hasty. Some studies indicate that nine days without fresh water seems to be their limit, but whether they need fresh lettuce or there is some other factor at work is not currently known.

Within Florida, manatees inhabit coastal areas, creeks, lagoons, and bays. They inhabit mostly shallow waters; anything deeper than three feet seems to be enough for them. Rarely will they venture into deep ocean water. It's not that they are weak swimmers; it's where they find seagrass, their main food source. But manatees are far from homebodies. In fact, they have no "territory" at all. They are nomadic, living placidly off the land, so to speak.

When the weather warms and adventure calls, the traveling sea cows nose their way eastward and southward to Cuba and the Bahamas, westward to the Texas and Louisiana coastline, and, in a spurt of derring-do that can get them into serious trouble, north to New Jersey and even Massachusetts. This can create a lot of headaches for rescue teams, if, as sometimes happens, manatees outstay their warm-water welcome. They have to be hauled out of the water, looked after, and sent home to Florida. (Manatees can be transported by search-and-rescue planes or by truck. They do not need to be submerged in water for the trip.)

Additionally, when in a marine environment, manatees are in the unfortunate habit of collecting barnacles. When the animals head back into fresh water, the barnacles soon fall off, leaving small roundish scars on the manatee's hide. The manatee's flaky, sheddable skin also helps remove the hitchhikers. No one wants barnacles attached to them.

Manatee Anatomy
(Broadly Speaking)

The first thing most people notice about manatees is how large they are. This is important since, as it turns out, size is their only defense. Still, somehow, it's unexpected. A run-of-the-mill manatee weighs in at half a ton and grows to about ten feet long, but a really big one can easily top three thousand pounds and attain thirteen feet, with females being somewhat larger than males.

Let's face it, manatees look fat! But this is an illusion. Their elegant fusiform shape is perfectly designed for their habitat and lifestyle. Their sleekly rotund look is not a result of overeating at all. The inside of that rotund middle is called "the gut tract," and it contains a big stomach and many yards of intestines. These are needed to hold and process a hundred pounds of seagrass a day. Though they have three-inch-thick skin, there's no continuous layer of blubber underneath it as dolphins or whales have. This relative fatlessness allows manatees to be comfortable only in tropical and subtropical regions. In fact, mid-Florida is the extreme northern point of their winter range, and even there, chilly waters can produce cold lesions on the sea cows.

Manatees also have an admirable set of axial muscles and thick ribs to complete the look. The fancy name for thick bones like these is "pachyostatic," which simply means "swollen." Their bones are heavy, hard, and solid (osteosclerotic). The long bones of most mammals are filled with marrow, the body's blood cell–making factory. Not manatees. They make their red blood cells in their sternum.

And, yes, it is true, manatees do not have necks. Every other mammal (except for the always fascinating sloth, a case study in itself) has seven cervical or neck bones. Manatees

The most fun part of manatee anatomy is the peduncle, the area between the body and the fluke. It's not only a great word to pronounce, but it seems to have been specially designed by God so that scientists can attach tracking tethers to it to keep an eye on the mysterious creature's movements.

Manatee flippers are flexible and quite useful. This one is delicately transferring food to its mouth.
Source: *Keith Ramos, USFWS ROYALTY FREE (PIXNIO-29336-2008x3000)*

have only six. (Their cousin the dugong can't seem to make up its mind about how many neck bones to have—some have six while others opt for the traditional seven.) At any rate, manatees cannot turn their heads, but must move their entire bodies to turn around and look at something, which they do with their lashless, lidless eyes.

FLIPPING FOR FLIPPERS (AND FLUKES)

Manatee flippers are long, jointed, and flexible, enabling their owners to steer easily, put food into their mouths, and crawl along the benthic surface. They can even use them to hug each other. If you had X-ray vision and aimed your sights on the manatee flipper, you'd see finger bones that very much resemble those of a human hand. (Toothed whales, seals, and sea lions have a similar arrangement.) There are, technically speaking, no hind limbs, but if you looked carefully, you'd find tiny unattached pelvic bones buried deep in the pelvic musculature.

The manatee tail, or fluke, is flat and paddle shaped, distinguishing it from its close cousin, the dugong, which has a deeply forked tail like a whale or dolphin.

Sadly, these same wondrous flippers can become irrevocably damaged by monofilament fishing line, which can cause the animal severe pain, permanent scarring, or even loss of a limb and, in some cases, resulting in death.

> Although some experts insist that the manatee tail is properly termed a "paddle" and that the word "fluke" be reserved for dolphins, I have seen the two terms used interchangeably throughout the literature and do so here.

COLOR MY MANATEE, OR GRAY IS THE NEW GRAY

Most manatees are gray, but some look brownish or even black, especially among the younger set: they lighten into gray as they develop. In any case, the color they appear to be is often dictated to some degree by the kind of algae or other material that has attached itself to the manatee's rough skin, either trailing delicately behind the animal as it swims or thriving in mosslike patches directly on the hide. As a general rule, the older the manatee gets, the more algae it acquires. It seems to be an arrangement of mutual benefit. The manatee provides the living quarters for the algae, and the algae may play a part in protecting the manatee from the sun's harmful rays when it basks on the surface of the water.

Possibly feeling desperate for unique new color tones, several companies have cashed in on the cachet of manatees. For example, the color "manatee gray" has now been immortalized by the Dixie Belle paint company, which advertises Manatee Gray Chalk Mineral Paint. In their own inimitable words on their website (https://dixiebellepaint .com/manatee-gray-chalk-paint): "Manatee Gray is a light gray with soft blue undertones. Just like the sweet sea creatures, this cool color will add a gentle energy to your home. Use this refreshing gray in your kitchen, dining room or guest bedroom and bath. You'll feel calmer than shallow ocean waves whenever you see this color." (And if you combine one part Manatee Gray with one part of Dixie Belle blue, you will end up with "Harbor Mist." Hard to see how you can go wrong with that.) Glidden paint also once had a manatee-colored paint: Manatee Grey (note the difference in spelling; I suppose they are trying to be very British and romantic). But Glidden Manatee Grey was a lot grayer (greyer?) than the Dixie Belle version.

Some Target customers, however, didn't get the same warm, fuzzy, gray feeling when the franchise decided to market a new dress as "manatee gray"—but only for plus-sized customers. Regular-sized buyers could purchase the same dress in "dark heather gray." The company apologized and decided to market the larger dresses as simply "gray." It also made a few incoherent remarks about manatee gray being a "seasonal color." As a side note, the larger sized dress was $2 cheaper. Other manatee gray products include Nucor Manatee Gray Ceruse Rigid Core Luxury Vinyl Plank. Even Crayola Crayons have an official "manatee." According to the experts, "manatee" is actually a shade of blue. In the RGB color model, it is comprised of 55.29 percent red, 56.47 percent green and 63.14 percent blue. It is not my fault that these add up to more than 100 percent. Manatees are big.

The fashion industry has also cashed in recently on something called "manatee blue." As described rather weirdly by Rebecca Storm of SSense, "It reaffirms its sluggish, temporal subsistence: the color of an afterglow, a dream, of smoke. If you watch footage of the California wildfires for longer than a minute, and then close your eyes, your fatigued cone cells will reveal flame orange's contrast complementary: Manatee Blue," which, she elaborates, is a "blue that is pale at times, distinctively murky at others, depending on how it's draped, photographed. The blue of 3D printed prototypes; of stonewashed primaries; of cigarette smoke; of industrial dye baths; of dirty, worn-out denim." She also says it is "shy." Okay. Enough of that. Let's move on.

A couple in South Dakota of all places started Manatee Party Tie Dyeing Company. (On their website, they refer to it as "tie-dying," which makes one feel slightly uncomfortable, but, hey, we all make typos.)

While we are in the world of products, I could mention Manatee Gourmet Coffee Caribbean Delight Whole Bean Coffee. Quite the noun cluster there. Anyway, it's a "rich medium roast with hints of coconut, hazelnut, and caramel." And since it is supported by the Save the Manatee Club, a wonderful organization dedicated to helping our sea cows, it's a coffee with a cause, so you should buy it. Good stuff. You can get it decaf or preground, if you like.

How Manatees Stay Warm

Manatees (and their cousins, the dugongs) are warm-water creatures. Despite their impressive resemblance to walruses, they can't handle water temperatures below 68 degrees Fahrenheit for a sustained period. Having neither blubber nor fur like other marine mammals, they are restricted to warm waters. In fact, the Florida manatee is at the very edge of its tolerated range. (The Antillean manatee is more southerly, inhabiting the milder waters off Guatemala, Belize, Honduras, Costa Rica, Panama, Nicaragua, Colombia, Venezuela, Guyana, Suriname, Brazil, Trinidad and Tobago, Jamaica, Cuba, Haiti, the Dominican Republic, Puerto Rico, and the Bahamas. Every once in a while, the Florida manatee makes its way over to the Bahamas as well, but it's not a common occurrence.)

During bitter cold snaps or long chilly winters, manatees are at great risk of cold stress, pneumonia, and even death. If exposed to even moderately cold water (temperatures below about 68 degrees) for very long, cold-stressed manatees may begin eating sporadically, having apparently lost their appetite. Severe or prolonged cold can slow the metabolism and even effect an immune system shutdown.

During periods of extreme cold with water temperatures below 61 degrees, manatees may stop eating entirely. This unfortunate development leads to a decrease in the little protective body fat they have and a lack of energy stores. And when they stop eating, there is no warming fermentation going on in the gut, which leads to even greater cold stress. They become emaciated, with a sunken area near the back of the head called, reasonably enough, a "peanut head."

A cold-stressed animal is lethargic and may have white patches of sloughed-off skin. These patches might be mistaken for typical manatee boat scars if you're not looking carefully, but closer examination reveal them as lesions. They most likely appear on the animal's extremities—flippers, fluke, or snout. Manatee researchers actually "score" these cold-stress lesions to document the severity of the animal's exposure to the cold. Such wounds have the unhappy nickname of "Florida frostbite." Cold-stressed manatees must be moved to warm, clean water and given nutritional supplementation, usually by

Several manatees glide silently and almost invisibly beneath the surface of this river. Their near invisibility is one factor that makes them vulnerable to boat strikes. Source: *Steve Hillebrand, USFWS ROYALTY FREE (PIXNIO-29358-3504x2336)*

Researchers measure a manatee's cortisol level to determine how much chronic stress, which leads to a weakened immune system, the animal is under due to prolonged cold. It was shown that indeed their immune systems did become depressed, leaving room for secondary and opportunistic infections from the papilloma virus, bacteria, and even fungi on the head, fluke, and flippers.

high-calorie tube feeding until the lesions heal and there is sufficient weight gain. Lesions may take months to heal. If a manatee needs antibiotics, they are usually delivered parenterally, since oral antibiotics give them diarrhea.

The winter of 2009–2010 was the coldest on record in manatee country, especially in the east-central regions, with temperatures on New Year's Day approaching arctic levels. Not only manatees, but fish, sea turtles, and corals suffered a major hit from acute hypothermia. This occurs when manatees leave warm water for cold-water immersion, a phenomenon that may be accompanied

Manatee are sometimes found off the coast of Texas, but no one knows if they originated from Florida or Mexico, and the manatees aren't telling anyone, possibly for fear of being asked for some sort of documentation.

by hyperventilation, heart arrhythmia, and weakness. The victims were mostly younger animals.

Technical terms describing the horrific effect on them include pustular dermatitis, in which, as the name indicates, pus-filled "pimples" form under the top layer of the skin. They may also suffer enterocolitis, an inflammation of the digestive tract, inflammation or degeneration of the heart muscle, and enlarged lymph nodes near the axillae (armpits). At one time, cold was the number one killer of manatees. In fact, there was probably little other check on their population growth. However, the advent of boat traffic and, catastrophically, the pollution-driven crash of the seagrass meadows have taken an even more severe toll upon them.

To escape death by freezing, come November, most manatees swarm into warm-water refuges (or, as researchers call them, "refugia." I shall use "refuges," however, as my native language is English). As anyone who has visited one of these places knows, "manatee density" can be very high there, with the sea cows cheek by jowl in an attempt to conserve heat. They generally leave as soon as the temperatures warm up. Between 15 and 18 percent of manatees head for four natural warm springs, their most ancient and most natural refuge. Florida has more natural warm springs than any other place on earth. These refuges are under constant pressure, however, as human beings continue to siphon off the groundwater that is the source of the springs. And, of course, the constant pressure of human development adds to pollution everywhere. (The extraction of so much water from the springs is also stressing Florida's aquifers, and salt water has been creeping into them. This bodes no good for anyone.)

The most popular natural winter refuges are (reasonably enough) in the south and central part of the state. The northernmost are at Crystal River and Blue Spring in the St. John's River, along the East Coast. There are no known natural warm springs in the southeast part of the state. However, there are also a lot of lesser known winter refuges, such as canals and boat basins.

Blue Spring State Park is a major success story. When the Save the Manatee Club manatee specialist Wayne Hartley began counting them in 1980, only thirty-six manatees wintered in the park. In 2022, a record 871 spent the winter there. Each of them has a name assigned by Hartley, sometimes according to a theme (Harry Potter characters during one phase), sometimes signifying a relationship to its mother if known. Each is also (more scientifically) assigned a number like Blue Spring 140.

It is believed that aboriginal peoples staked out these warm springs as killing grounds for manatees, who are easy to catch and kill under such conditions.

Between 48 and 60 percent of manatees occupy areas containing warm-water discharges (outfalls) from ten power plants. The outfalls produce water temperatures that happen to be just right for manatee winter survival. They can be observed in such areas in great numbers in places such as Florida Power and Light's Manatee Lagoon, which also hosts educational programs about Florida sea cows. Indeed, power plants are one of manatees' primary means of survival since the loss of their natural refuges.

Power plant refuges are a comparatively recent feature of manatee life, within the last fifty years. Over time, as word got around, the number of manatees using them has increased. Currently, power plants identified as providing critical manatee habitat are required by law to implement a "manatee protection plan" that speaks to the consistency and temperature of warm-water discharges in the winter. Unlike warm springs, which remain at a constant temperature throughout the year, discharge temperatures can fluctuate considerably at power plants. When temperatures dip into the teens, which can happen in the northern and even central parts of the state, power plants are often unable to raise discharge temperatures sufficiently to prevent manatee cold stress. (To be fair to power plants, keeping manatees warm was not their original mission.)

Thus, power plants are not an ideal solution for keeping manatees both warm and fed. Many of the power plant refuges simply have no available food. And manatees are trapped there by the walls of frigid water around them and calves nurse their mothers dry. Even those that live through the winter can be so weak that their long-term survival is doubtful.

In addition, all the manatee power plant refuges are aging due to outdated technologies and high costs. Many will go offline within the next twenty years or so. This is a serious threat to manatee survival, especially considering the manatees' commitment (site fidelity) to a particular refuge. (Word apparently gets around in manatee circles, and calves seem, unsurprisingly, to learn this behavior from their mothers.) Although we might consider this a good thing—and certainly a clever adaptation on the part of manatees—there are dangers. For example, many manatees in more northern areas used to migrate south during the winter. Many of them now hang around the power plant all winter, becoming increasingly dependent on them. They may have forgotten where to migrate to, should the power plant go offline.

Evidence that this is true is suggested by events during the winter of 1998–1999. An artificial warm-water discharge on Amelia Island in north Florida had to be modified to meet water quality standards by moving it to deeper water. Since manatees inhabit only shallow waters, it became unavailable to them for winter warming. State and federal agencies agreed to the move because only a small number of manatees were using it, and it also afforded an opportunity for an interesting research project essential for future manatee protection: what would the manatees do when their winter spa disappeared? On November 10, the warm-water discharge was turned off. Researchers who hoped the manatees would migrate south were disappointed. Most of the manatees who used the site did not migrate, and several died from cold stress. Some tried to find secondary sites in Georgia, but these unfortunately did not supply enough warm water for their needs. The indubitable fact is that although artificial refuges are certainly not natural, manatees have become dependent on them. This is a problem that human beings have created and that we must solve.

Subadults are the most commonly affected by the cold. Younger calves are possibly given protection by their mothers; certainly, their fat-rich milk diet is protective in cold weather.

A different kind of power plant problem emerged in February 1997, when a big brouhaha was raised about the construction of a Florida Power and Light power plant. Interestingly, objections first came from the Southwest Florida Marine Trade Association (SWFMTA). It claimed (correctly) that the power plant would disrupt historic migration patterns for manatees. Instead of heading south, they would just hang out at the power plant all winter. The SWFMTA might not normally give a hoot, but in this case, it brought up the fact that this area has high boat traffic, which would undoubtedly lead to disastrous collisions (and of course more manatee "speed zones"). Additionally, it would concentrate manatees in an area with historically high levels of deadly red tide. Although the permit challenge was settled in March 1998, the problem is ongoing.

About 35 percent of counted manatees, however, use no known warm-water source or else take advantage of passive thermal basins (PTBs) that may trap warm water for a week or so. There are two types of PTBs. Most of these are deep basins that are warmed by the sun throughout the day and cool slowly overnight. Others are comprised of warm salty water trapped under a layer of fresh water flowing from upstream runoff.

Currently, officials divide winter refuges into three classes: (1) high quality refuges (mostly springs) that maintain water temperatures at greater than 72 degrees Fahrenheit in all weather conditions; (2) medium quality refuges (mostly power plants and some PTBs that remain above 72 degrees in mild winter conditions but can fall to 68 degrees during severe cold; and (3) low quality refuges (mostly PTBs and power plants that operate intermittently) that remain above 68 degrees in mild winters but have no reliable warm water in severe cold.

Refuges are literally lifesavers. Young manatees learn where to find them from their mothers during the first year of their lives, and many retain remarkable "site fidelity" to these areas throughout their lives. The Florida Fish and Wildlife Conservation Commission is working to protect and enhance existing natural refuges to keep manatees warmer and more comfortable. Natural refuges are much better for manatees anyway, since discharges from power plants can fluctuate wildly. Natural springs maintain the same temperature year-round, usually around 72 degrees. Brisk but bearable.

Aside from warm-water refuges, manatees are not completely helpless in the face of cold. Like most marine mammals, manatees are big, which serves to aid in keeping them warm. They also have a few tricks up their flippers: internally, the bacteria in their digestive system breaks down the cellulose in their diet, releasing warming energy. It helps a little. Their delicious roundness, reflecting the furnace inside them, is a testament to this heat-making ability. Their fellow subspecies, the Antillean manatee, is packed into a sleeker and smaller frame, as it does not face the colder weather that Florida manatee do.

To keep warm, manatees often bask on the surface of the water on sunny winter days, which unfortunately can get them into a different kind of trouble: it puts them at greater risk of getting struck by a boat.

Interestingly, studies done on captive manatees (Hugh and Buffett of Mote Marine Laboratory) in 2018 showed that despite exposure to constant water temperature throughout the year, the sea cows had significantly lower heat flux in winter than in summer. (Much more about Hugh and Buffett to come.)

Furthermore, like their fellow sea mammals (and even some sea reptiles such as leather-back turtles), manatees are blessed with "counter-current heat exchangers" in their "arm-pits" (axillae), flippers, and at the base of their fluke (or as we say in the manatee business, their caudal peduncle. I try never to miss a chance to write or say the word "peduncle."). This means that many of their veins and arteries are skillfully placed so that their arterial blood stays well away from the surface of their bodies where the body heat could be diffused away by the chilly water, thus maintaining core temperature.

Though cold is the enemy of all manatees, it is interesting that some individuals can withstand cold stress much better than others. Indeed, some manatees seem so well-equipped to endure the cold that they never bother retreating into warm-water refuges at all. In this way, as in so many others, manatees are like people who also have vary-ing degrees of tolerance for the cold. Factors that enable some manatees to survive may include surface area–to-volume ratio and size (bigger is better in some cases, after all), general health condition, amount of fat insulation, and nutritional status.

Death from cold stress is not uncommon and is even considered "natural," a dodgy conclusion in my opinion, since human beings have made many of their natural warm-water refuges unavailable to them. At any rate, a cold-stressed manatee should be reported to the authorities so that it can be rescued, warmed up, and returned to its natural environment when temperatures ameliorate. However, it appears to be the case that after a serious cold-stress event, a manatee's immune system is compromised, perhaps for many months or even years afterward. (It's difficult to truly test this kind of thing, but that currently seems to be the consensus.)

Ocean's Breath (A Brief Nod to Yoga)

How Manatees Breathe

Manatees are mammals, and like all mammals, need to breathe air, even though they spend most of their time under water. Unlike dolphins and whales, manatees do not possess a blowhole. (In case you're wondering, the blowhole is opened by muscles when the animal surfaces and closes from the pressure of water when it dives again.) Manatees, on the other hand, sport a handsome pair of valved nostrils at the tips of their heads. These nostrils close automatically when they submerge.

Unlike us, manatees are not automatic breathers. They need to "think" to take a breath, just as we need to think to hold ours. Completely different system. The amount of time a manatee spends under water depends on how active it is. A vigorously swimming manatee takes a breath every three to five minutes, whereas a resting one need come up only every twenty minutes. It also partly depends on size, with larger, older animals able to submerge longer than younger and smaller ones.

When they are asleep, the rib cage muscles relax automatically, allowing the manatee to drift to the surface to take a breath. With every breath, manatees change 90 percent of the air in their lungs. This amount of air exchange is higher than that of any other mammal, including dolphins, who check in at about 80 percent. Human beings, for example, change only 10 percent. When a manatee does surface, the exhalation explodes from the nostrils with a sound loud enough to alert the immediate neighborhood. If you're out minding your own business, paddling around on your kayak, for instance, the sudden whoosh of a manatee expelling its breath will get your attention. After the manatee takes a breath, the rib muscles contract, allowing the animal to sink quietly beneath the surface again.

Since manatees are mammals, we can expect that they have lungs. They do, but like everything else about manatees, their three-foot lungs are very unusual, stretching nearly two-thirds the length of their bodies to aid in buoyancy. They're aligned along the backbone (horizontal or dorsal plane) rather than along the rib cage (transverse plane) like the rest of us. This design allows them to float effortlessly. In fact, some people have compared

Manatees can swim upside down with perfect ease (so there, dolphins!). Notice the flipper nails, reminiscent of when manatee ancestors roamed the earth. Amazonian manatees do not have flipper nails. Source: *Jim P. Reid, USFWS ROYALTY FREE (PIXNIO-29344-3593x2400)*

manatee lungs to flotation tanks. Unlike the case in almost all other mammals, each lung resides in its own separate cavity and diaphragm. These extremely muscular structures are called "hemidiaphragms," each of which can contract separately. The diaphragm does not separate the heart from the liver as it does in all other mammalian orders.

The diaphragm does not attach to the sternum, either, but at the I-shaped central tendon to bony projections extending ventrally from the vertebrae. The orientation and power of the lungs enable sea cows to change position in the water with no visible effort as they move up and down the water column, roll, and pitch with ease.

In case you're wondering how scientists know so much about manatee breathing, we have Mote Marine Laboratory in Sarasota, Florida, and its resident manatee half brothers, Hugh and Buffett, to thank. Researchers placed a resuscitator mask attached to a Spirometrics PC Flow spirometer on the manatee, which measures the volume and flow rates of each breath. The manatees were rewarded for taking increasingly larger breaths so that true vital lung capacity could be measured. Luckily for the researchers, manatees are highly tolerant about being messed around with like this. And if they get too annoyed, they just swim away. Hugh and Buffett have actually been trained to wait until a mask is placed before taking a breath.

HUGH AND BUFFET: A BRIEF INTERLUDE

Hugh and Buffett are the only two manatees in the world who have been trained to participate in experiments designed to learn more about this intriguing species. Buffett was named after singer-songwriter Jimmy Buffett, a cofounder of the Save the Manatee Club. Hugh was named after—well—Hugh-Manatee. Get it? Okay. Hugh, the elder brother, was born June 28, 1984, at the Miami Seaquarium. His proud parents are Romeo and Lorelei. Currently Hugh weighs about thirteen hundred pounds. He is 9.7 feet long and his umbilical girth has been measured at 6.6 feet. Some time ago, Hugh developed abscesses on his shoulder, which had to be surgically removed, leaving him with a couple of very handsome scars. Although he has lived at several aquaria throughout Florida, he has never been released to the wild. He is described by his keepers at Mote Marine as a "very active" manatee swimming vigorously most of the day (and eating while he swims). They attribute his comparative svelteness to his intense physical activity. His favorite toy is reported to be an ice float. The ice float is simply a plastic tub filled with water and apples, carrots, and kale, which is then frozen. A cooling snack is always a treat. It bobs along the surface of the water. Hugh rolls onto his back and clutches the tub with his pectoral flippers and munches away.

Buffett, the younger brother, was born May 16, 1987, also in Miami Seaquarium. His faithless father was also Romeo, but his mom was Juliet, not the aforementioned Lorelei. He is much lazier than Hugh but more people-oriented, spending a good portion of the day staring at visitors through the glass divider that separates him from them. Scientists have recruited Buffett, along with Hugh, for various research projects, and as a result his activity level (and presumably his happiness) has increased. Buffett weighs about 1,776 pounds. He is 10.3 feet long and his girth is 8.3 feet.

The two incarcerated manatees are fed a daily diet of 120 heads of romaine lettuce, 12 bunches of kale, and plenty of treats. One of the treats includes beets. I keep wondering who the first person was to suggest that manatees might like beets. The manatees also receive three multivitamins per day, snuck into a monkey-chow snack.

To spice up their otherwise rather drab existence, the scientists at Mote Marine have implanted a number of "environmental enrichment devices" for their permanent residents. Creating the right ones can be a challenge. Think of Hugh and Buffett as giant toddlers. The toys must not be swallowable. Therefore, they can't be breakable, since once broken they could be swallowed. They also can't have sharp parts that could stab the manatee, or worse, entangle the animal.

Current favorites include:

- a back scratcher consisting of four industrial-strength shop brooms attached to PVC pipe
- a hula hoop, size extra large, mostly worn around the "neck"
- a ten-feet-long vacuum hose partially filled with water, which is carried around the tank

- a sixteen-by-eighteen-inch section of plastic grating suspended just below the surface of the water, which manatees like to rub their faces against
- a kale feeder made of a large PVC pipe drilled with holes and stuffed with kale

Mote Marine Laboratory has a place on its website where people can submit their own ideas for manatee toys. If they use your idea, you will receive your very own photograph with the manatees and your toy. Even better, they will put the photo on the website's Environmental Enrichment Device Photo Gallery. One thing they will not do is pay you. Or let you swim with the manatees.

How Manatees Swim
(Eat Your Heart Out, Michael Phelps)

When I was volunteering at the Manatee Observation and Education Center in Fort Pierce, Florida, one day, a young visitor asked me if manatees could swim. Her teacher had grandly informed her that manatees could not swim but only float like jellyfish. I had to tell her that not only do manatees swim, but that jellyfish do, too, contracting the muscles in their "bell" to expel water and propel them forward. (If you've been around for five hundred million years, you learn a trick or two.)

Manatees are in fact champion swimmers. Don't let their bloblike appearance deceive you. They can swim upside down. They can swim vertically. They can somersault and barrel roll. They can also swim for many miles. One, the famous Chessie, was recorded as traveling three thousand miles, at about twelve to fourteen miles per day.

Manatees propel themselves through water using their powerful flukes. They are often regarded as slow swimmers, typically drifting along at about five miles per hour. However, that seems speedy when we consider that the fastest human swimmers can manage only just over five miles per hour using maximum effort. With a flip of its fluke, a manatee can zip along at twenty miles an hour for brief periods, usually to escape danger. They are also rather fond of body surfing, an activity usually started by one manatee and then copied by others, apparently simply for the joie de vivre of the thing.

To stay afloat at any depth is a tricky business, for which manatees possess a number of adaptations. One way is by contracting or expanding their powerful diaphragms and thus changing the volume in their lungs. The fact that the long lungs lie on a transverse plane makes buoyancy even easier.

The solidity of manatee bones provide them with the negative buoyancy they need for cruising along the bottom of their habitat cropping seagrass. On the other hand, their fat contributes to a positive buoyancy, making everything add up to neutral. This clever combination allows sea cows to hover nearly motionless anywhere in the water column. (Try this and see what happens to you.) This is really important, since it allows manatees to spend as much time as they like cropping the seagrass at the bottom without effort.

Two manatees nuzzle on the benthic surface. Perhaps they are exchanging gossip or maybe just looking for food. Source: *Jim P. Reid, USFWS ROYALTY FREE (PIXNIO-29330-3593x2400)*

This seeming effortlessness, however, must be learned by the calves, who often perform a rather comical and awkward series of maneuvers to stay close to (and at the same depth as) their mothers.

Their most interesting buoyancy technique is the storage and release of digestive gases. In fact, the telltale fart bubbles in the water often give away their presence to curious manatee seekers. The Florida manatee collects these fart gases in intestinal pockets. The more gas that is stored, the higher they float. Releasing the gases strategically allows them to sink, and a constipated manatee can be in big trouble, unable to dive to reach food. Normally, manatees seem able to move up and down the water column effortlessly.

The subject of manatee farts is apparently such a hot topic, so to speak, that Snopes .com saw fit to take up the issue and settle the controversy: "Do Manatees Control Their Buoyancy by Farting?" (February 9, 2021). This article was published during the height of the COVID-19 pandemic, when people were locked up at home with little to do but think about farting manatees. At any rate, they labeled the claim "true," for whatever that's worth. The same article also casually mentioned that manatees were the "only completely herbivorous aquatic mammal," conveniently forgetting dugongs. (Besides, manatees will eat animal protein if it's mixed up in their seagrass. They're not really picky.)

By the way, manatees, unlike dolphins and whales, can not only swim, but also can walk on their flexible jointed flippers. In fact, manatee can use their flippers for feeding. Each flipper can move independently to gather quite a large amount of food to shovel in their mouths. (Florida manatees also have three or four nails at the end of each flipper, giving that appendage a definite elephant-like appearance.)

Inevitably, this brings us to the topic of commercial "swimming with manatees" at Three Sisters Springs, a tourist attraction in Crystal River, Florida, and a big moneymaker for the locals. Three Sisters Springs is one of Florida's last remaining urban springs, and every year, at least 250,000 boaters, divers, snorkelers, and swimmers flock to the area, putting pressure on both Three Sisters Springs and the animals who live there. People seem to have an ingrained desire to swim with, pet, and interact with manatees. Some manatees seem to enjoy the interactions, a few going so far as to glide up to the divers and hug them. However, others flee from people, huddling in cordoned-off "safe" areas while kayakers and snorkelers stake them out, waiting for them to emerge (since the safe areas often have no food available). It can be a disturbing sight—dozens of manatees trying to hide from their stalkers. The truth is that manatees are best left alone, especially in winter, when swimming away drains their energy in the cold water. It is for this reason that swimming with manatees is not regular entertainment in Florida, except for Crystal River, where it has been grandfathered in. As a result, dozens of companies offer manatee sightseeing and swimming tours, increasing the number of boat propellers in the water, ripping up the fragile seagrass.

In my opinion, true manatee aficionados will forgo the feel-good experience of swimming with them and leave the sea cows to their own devices. On the other hand, it is admittedly a magical experience when one unexpectedly nudges you when you're just wading around minding your own business. Or, as happened to me once, when a manatee pushes your kayak around for twenty minutes before getting bored and drifting away.

How Manatees Feel (Not Slimy Except When Covered with Algae)

Manatees have been called "tactile specialists" with good reason. They have whiskers (bristles) all over their bodies, although the face is about 30 percent hairier than the rest of the body. It was once thought that only sea cows were so adorned; however, it has been recently discovered that at least some hyraxes (who belong to the same clade as manatees) also possess whiskers over the entire body. It has therefore been suggested that the common ancestor of manatees and hyraxes also possessed this unusual feature. The evocatively named naked mole-rats have about 40 of them them as well, a discovery that should result in a name change, perhaps to something like "tactile-haired mole-rats." Just touch one of those bristles and the mole-rat will immediately snap its snout around to find out what's happening. Since we have no fossil evidence, mammalogists are waiting for molecular developmental studies to learn more.

In manatees, three thousand body whiskers are evenly spaced every two or three inches, containing twenty to fifty nerve fibers each. Unlike ordinary hair, the antenna-like manatee whiskers are used to gather information about the environment. Much more useful than plain nerveless hair. The bristles are embedded in a specialized follicle, each with its own separate blood supply. Each connects to a dense, intricate nerve network (more than two hundred thousand nerves involved here) that can transmit tactile information to the brain. About 25 percent of the manatee brain is devoted to the somatosensory cortex. Technically, only the whiskers on the lips are called vibrissae. Everywhere else, they are just bristles. These vibrissae are as sensitive as human fingertips, and each is connected to

Vibrissae in general seem to contribute to lots of behaviors in several species. They have a role in facial expression for intraspecies communications, scattering pheromones, maintaining head position in swimming, and a whole lot of environmental monitoring, like detecting water current (and wind direction for land animals).

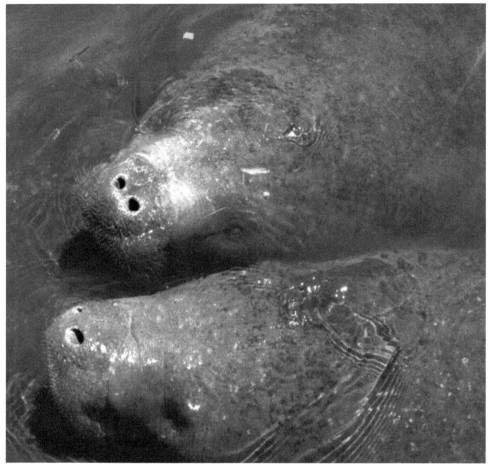

Although manatees have a thick, tough hide, they have little blubber and are susceptible to cold. They crowd together for warmth. Source: *Dr. Beth Brady, Mote Marine Laboratory*

a separate cluster of cells in the brain. In fact, it might be useful to think of manatees as having fingers on their faces. Horrifying, perhaps, but useful. To test the sensitivity of the vibrissae, Hugh and Buffett were trained to use only their whiskers, not their vision, to decide which target of two presented had the wider grooves and ridges. Not to be trusted to keep their eyes closed when commanded, the brothers were blindfolded and asked to press the wider striped target.

The bristles on their backs, for instance, may detect changes in current (pressure waves), temperature, and movement of other animals. They seem to be surrounded by mechanoreceptors to detect motion. If a hair is pushed aside by some environmental factor, the mechanoreceptor is squeezed and the nerve cells are activated. This system is similar to how a breeze feels on human skin or body hair but much, much more sensitive and can operate over much longer distances. Unfortunately, however, this system was not designed to detect anything moving as fast as a boat, which puts the manatee in peril.

There are more bristles on the top (dorsal) side than on the belly (ventral) side. Some researchers have compared the purpose of this distribution to the lateral line in fish. Manatees sometimes appear to use these hairs instead of vision to investigate objects of interest, water currents, or potential danger, sort of like antennae. Technically, this is called an "underwater distance tactile system." So far as we know, manatees are the only mammals to possess it. Even the lightest touch on one of these hairs elicits a response from the giant animal, flexing its hide or shifting away.

In 2017, Joseph Gaspard, director of animal health, science, and conservation at the Pittsburgh Zoo and PPG Aquarium, decided the hairs were worth studying. "Pumping blood to the surface to supply 3,000-plus hairs across the body? That's an expensive endeavor," he mused. It was long known that the whiskers were particularly useful for actively exploring and evaluating the environment ("active touch" sensitivity). Now it was time to check out the body hairs for their "passive touch" sensitivity, or response to that environment. The subjects were, unsurprisingly, the ever-tolerant Hugh and Buffett of Mote Marine Laboratory.

Gaspard and his fellow researchers built a vibration-proof box that enclosed a detector and placed it next to the manatee's flank hairs. They then directed tiny, focused waves at the hairs. The manatees had been trained to touch a target with their noses when they felt anything. Sure enough, the manatees were able to feel even the slightest perturbations. But was it really the hairs and not the skin? Gaspard needed to know. Grabbing his Wahl mustache and beard trimmer, he gave his subjects a buzz cut. The manatee's naturally wrinkly skin made a perfectly clean shave impossible. The trimming left short stubble. Apparently, it's well-nigh impossible for a sea cow to get a clean shave anywhere. The test was repeated, and the animals did three times less well, although they still could detect a whole lot—undoubtedly due to the remaining stubble. The results were published in the *Journal of Comparative Physiology*.

The facial whiskers are so perfectly developed that manatees can use them—in conjunction with the prehensile lips—to collect food, shift it around, and carry it to their mouths—exactly like their cousin, the elephant, uses its single mighty trunk. In fact, the bristles can feel things as delicately as an elephant can feel with its trunk. They have even been seen using their lips and bristles to remove unwanted sediment from the seagrasses they eat.

How Manatees See Their World

In cartoon drawings, manatee eyes are often depicted as large, soft, and adorned with curling eyelashes. In reality, manatee eyes are smallish, about half the size of ours (less than an inch in diameter), and lack eyelashes. However, they do have muscles around their eye that contract to close the eye, sort of like a camera lens. They also possess a third eyelid, or nictitating membrane, for protection.

The eyes of manatees are characterized as "avascular," meaning that there are no blood vessels in the cornea. This adaptation is not shared by other marine mammals like dolphins, and some researchers believe it functions to protect the eye in fresh water, upon which manatees are dependent for survival.

Scientists disagree about how well manatees can see. The perceived wisdom is that manatees have rather poor eyesight, but some recent research disputes this, depending on what is meant by "poor." In clear water, they seem to be able to perceive objects at a distance of about thirty-five yards. They also can see out of the water and often raise their heads to have a look around. In regard to far- or nearsightedness, most researchers believe that manatees have a normal range of vision or that they may be a bit farsighted.

Life can get boring in a tank, so Hugh and Buffet are often up for testing to break the monotony. For this experiment, the researchers used two squares of material covered in vertical stripes. The "control square" had very narrow stripes (about one millimeter) and the test square had wider stripes. The squares were suspended in the water about three feet from the manatees. Both manatees were trained to swim toward the target with the

Most of this experimental work has been done on two manatees, Hugh and Buffett, at Mote Marine Laboratory. Before they can do research with manatees, scientists have to get a permit from the US Fish and Wildlife Service. This was Permit # PRT-837923 in case you're interested.

Nostrils open wide for a deep breath. Manatees can remain under water for twenty minutes without surfacing, but active manatees take a breath every three to five minutes. Source: Steve Hillebrand, USFWS ROYALTY FREE (PIXNIO 29346-3504x2336)

wider stripes, avoiding the narrow-striped control target. The decision had to be made from at least a yard away.

The researchers gradually reduced the width of the stripes. When the manatees no longer seemed able to determine the difference between the correct target and the control, researchers applied a formula to determine the minimum angle of resolution (MAR) of the manatee's visual acuity.

Hugh and Buffett exhibited differences in this area, with Buffett outperforming Hugh by quite a lot. The results may be due to some idiosyncratic natural differences between the two subjects, or possibly they were just kidding around. Both manatees did less well than a legally blind human, although it must be said that Buffett edged out a cow but lost out to a frog.

We know manatees can distinguish some colors, since their retinas contain both rods and two types of cone receptors. (This is unusual among marine mammals. Most of them can see only shades of black and white.) Indeed, analyses of manatee eyes show a strong resemblance to those of their elephant cousins.

When I was researching this section of the book, I came across Manatee Family Eyecare. My first thought was, "How lovely! Caring for the vision of our state marine mammals," before I figured out that they were probably referring to human beings living in Manatee County, Florida.

Possibly, manatee eyes are best adapted to seeing patches of healthy green vegetation in a watery environment. Experiments show that manatees can tell blue and green from gray. Reds, however, and blue-green seem to flummox them. Vision of this sort is called dichromatic, meaning only two pigments are involved.

To test their ability to see brightness, scientists exposed four experimental subjects to thirty different shades of gray. They were only about one-third as good as we are at distinguishing these colors (as far as we can tell) but on par with fur seals. Apparently fur seals were subjected to the same experiment.

Florida manatees seem to be able to see in both day and nighttime conditions, although their Amazonian cousins, being more strictly nocturnal, possess mostly rods rather than cones. This makes sense, since their environment is generally pretty murky, making daytime seem like night.

Manatees also appear to have at least some binocular vision. They often stare at objects head-on, and there seems to be a slight overlap in the "ocular fields." As mentioned earlier, if manatees were human beings, they would be classified as legally blind. This doesn't matter so much since the sea cows can satisfy all their basic needs by relying on their other senses, especially those whiskers. But it is wrong to sneer at them for their eyesight. After all, human beings regularly mistook manatees for mermaids.

How Manatees Hear

Manatee ears are not visible to the casual onlooker (although you can find the external ear openings if you look about an inch behind the eyes), but that doesn't stop them from hearing everything. Their acoustical ability is exceptionally well-developed and occupies a large portion of their brain. Their large ear bones are well developed from birth. This is important, since mother manatees use sound to communicate with their young ones. Naturally, most of their hearing is directed for underwater use, but manatees can also hear sounds carried by air. Scientists believe that sound is transmitted though the fat/oil-filled jaw and carried to the ear bones. They hear about ten times better than we do under water (but only about half as well as dolphins).

Animals have an astounding range of abilities when it comes to hearing sounds. Marine mammals are traditionally divided into five "hearing groups" based on their range of best underwater hearing. There are "low frequency" animals, like blue and other baleen whales (7–35 kHz); midfrequency toothed whales, including most dolphins and sperm whales (150–160 kHz); high frequency toothed whales like some other dolphins and porpoises (275 Hz–160 kHz); most seals (50 Hz–86 kHz); and finally fur seals and sea lions (60 Hz–39 kHz).

Manatees detect high-frequency noises between 16,000 and 18,000 Hz (16–18 kHz) the best. Still, some studies show that manatees have a greater

Sound can be thought of as traveling in waves, similar to water waves. The distance from one wave crest to the next is the wavelength, the number of wave crests passing a fixed point in one second is the frequency. The more waves per second, the higher the pitch of the sound. Frequency, either sound or light, is measured in hertz (Hz). One hertz equals one cycle per second. The hertz is named for Heinrich Hertz, a nineteenth-century German physicist who established that light and radio waves (electromagnetic radiation) traveled in waves. Higher frequencies may be measured in kilohertz (kHz), so one kHz equals one thousand cycles per second.

sensitivity to low frequency sound than any marine mammal that has been studied to date. However, as studies by Edmund Gerstein and others show, manatees can hear a wide range of frequencies, including that of a motorboat moving at slow speed. One study found that manatees could follow signals changing at rates up to 1,400 Hz, with peaks in their response at 150 and 600 Hz. Although manatees mostly dwell in shallow water, where physical barriers inhibit the transmission of low frequency sounds (including that emitted by boat motors), they apparently can hear infrasound (frequencies too low for human ears) as well.

Scientists studying Hugh and Buffett discovered that the brothers could detect frequencies between 8 and 32 kHz very well. (For people, it's about 20 Hz to 20 kHz.) Buffett's hearing seemed especially acute; he could hear frequencies as high as 90.5 kHz, at which point he politely declined to participate in further experiments, snubbing his food rewards. He may have been annoyed by the sounds, but perhaps he was just bored.

Although manatees can't tell us how they feel about boat noise, it has been shown that, all else being equal, manatees prefer to dine in quiet areas away from the sounds of watercraft. If, as is typical, boating activity is heavier in the morning, manatees tend to arrive later in the day. What they seem to hate more than anything is the noise from "personal watercraft" like jet skis and "water scooters." Thus, manatees demonstrate their impeccable good taste.

In some South American cultures, it's considered a compliment to "have ears like a manatee." Indeed, some indigenous societies prize the stapes (inner ear bones) as talismans of great and holy significance, conferring power to their possessor. (Manatee ear bones are not unique in this regard. Some indigenous California tribes used dolphin or even fish ear bones as magical amulets.)

Some researchers are trying to create a sound system to save manatee lives. They developed a submerged alarm system that transmits a high-frequency sound from the bow of the boat, warning manatees to skedaddle. Manatees reacted to boat alarms thirty-nine out of forty-one times, swimming away from the high-pitched frequencies. However, there's a problem with this idea. In the first place, a manatee would have to have at least one bad encounter with the device-carrying boat before it could make a connection. This is called negative reinforcement conditioning. And if a large number of boats carried the devices, the "educated" manatee might not know how to respond and could even head in the direction of a boat not carrying the device. It would be nicer if boaters simply drove more slowly or, preferably from the manatee's viewpoint, just stayed at home and watched TV or played croquet (a vastly underappreciated sport).

Manatee ear bones also provide an important piece of information to researchers. By counting the annual growth rings in the ear bone, we can learn the manatee's age. In fact, this is the only way we can tell how old a manatee was when it died. Unfortunately, this can only be done after the animal has gone to the great lagoon in the sky.

How Manatees Communicate

Everyone knows by now all the great work that has been done studying the "language" of dolphins, those stars of the sea—or at least of SeaWorld. Much less is known about how manatees communicate, at least until recently, when Dr. Beth Brady and her colleagues undertook to study it. Brady listened to and analyzed 1,114 calls for this project (which is quite a lot, really), which were collected from three different manatee habitats around the state. The study was published in *The Journal of the Acoustical Society of America* during the plague year of 2020.

Manatees make noise using their vocal folds. Despite the size of the average manatee, however, all that comes out is a squeak or squeal. But despite lacking the loud trumpeting of their closest terrestrial cousins, the elephants, they manage to make themselves understood among *those who matter*.

Brady categorized manatee chitchat into five "call categories" based on visual inspection of spectrograms taken from hydrophones. Some work of this kind had been done earlier, but much of it was based on subjective determination. Brady quantified her observations using seventeen acoustic parameters, as well as "regression trees" (CARTs) and model-based cluster analysis paired with silhouette coefficients. "CART analysis revealed that these five broad call categories can be successfully distinguished based on correct classification scores of 41.6 to 62.5 percent. Silhouette coefficients determined that the manatee vocal repertoire is highly intergraded." Those are Beth's words. I can't make this stuff up. In simpler terms, she found that manatee calls can be divided into five different types, which she was able to represent visually on a spectrogram. The most common was the simple "squeak," but there was also the "high squeak" and the harsher "squeal," employed mainly when the manatee was playing or otherwise excited. It seems rather an anticlimactic noise for such massive animals. The bald eagle has the same problem. Its cry is so un-eaglelike that some moviemakers dub in the far more impressive sound of a red-tailed hawk. Most people don't notice.

How Manatees Smell (Not Great)

We are talking of course about how well manatees can perceive odors, a process that seems to involve the olfactory and taste senses as well as chemoreception. If we look at the manatee brain, we find that only a tiny, tiny portion of that organ is designated to sniff out the environment. In fact, its relative size is among the smallest among mammals. Still, olfactory tissue on small internal nasal bones has been found, and manatees have been observed rubbing against certain objects dubbed "marking stones," which may be used as an odor signal to other manatees—something to do with mating perhaps. Bull (male) manatees at least seem to respond to chemical "cues" in the urine of their lady friends, although no one is sure exactly how; it's been postulated that the transfer occurs via "retronasal delivery" to the epithelium or taste buds, although other scientists are doubtful about this, citing a tricky valve at the base of the nasal canal. "The manatee would need to have excellent control of this valve to allow aqueous solutions to pass from the oropharanx and through the nasopharanx to the olfactory epithelium at a minimum volume of water," helpfully explains researcher Meghan Lee Bills (Barboza) in her thesis, "Description of the Chemical Senses of the Florida Manatee, *Trichechus manatus latirostris* in Relation to Reproduction."

Manatee anal glands hold equal interest. (It was discovered only recently that manatees even have anal glands.) They are apparently used as potential source of chemosensory signal. We also know that gland size and "productivity" increase with the season.

It also has been suggested that manatees use taste chemoreception to orient themselves over long distances. For local conditions, they depend on their wonderful bristles.

How Manatees Sleep

Manatees spend half the day sleeping. I could stop there, but there's more to manatee sleeping than it may appear. When sleeping, manatees close their eyes (with their circular eyelids), but when they rise to the surface to breathe during sleep, they open them. Like other marine mammals (and birds), manatees have evolved unihemispheric sleep, in which half of the brain rests while the other half remains "awake." They switch roles every several minutes. This enables manatees to rise to the surface to breathe even when they are asleep. They obviously need to be at least partially awake to perform the motor functions they

The manatee tail (fluke) is flat and paddle-shaped, distinguishing it from its close cousin, the dugong, which has a forked tail like a whale or dolphin. Source: *Dr. Beth Brady, Mote Marine Laboratory*

need to rise to the surface, breathe, and return to their resting place. (Human beings sleep bihemispherically, with both halves of the brain asleep at the same time.) No one really knows how unihemispheric sleep works, but scientists think it involves a complex interaction between the hypothalamus, basal forebrain, and brain stem. The neural mechanisms supporting wakefulness dominate one side of the brain, while those promoting sleep control the other side. Unihemispheric sleepers don't seem to need as much sleep as the rest of us, either. Very little work has been done on this aspect of manatee behavior, possibly because the scientists couldn't stay awake long enough to do it.

Birds are even more amazing. A migrating bird can sleep while flying—the awake/non-awake parts of the brain switching sides every few seconds. On the other hand, they can also sleep bihemispherically if they are perched and safe. Seals likewise seem to be able to choose which mode of sleep they prefer at any given time.

Manatees can rest in any position or place but seem to prefer lounging around in holes or depressions in the seabed floor where the currents are slow.

When I began to research manatee sleep habits, I started to wonder if they dream. Then I got sidetracked thinking about what it means if humans dream about manatees. I learned that dream manatees represent emotion and one's feminine, peaceable side. On the negative side, it could mean that you are being too passive in a stressful situation. If you dream about multiple manatees, it means that you need to take a break in your life; you need to relax more.

Speaking of dreaming manatee dreams, people have composed several strange, dreamlike, and peculiar songs about manatees. There's some instrumental music called "Dream of the Manatee" by Neal Hellman and Joe Weed. There's another one titled "Manatee Dreams of Neptune" by Kat Epple and Bob Stohl. You can listen to either or both on YouTube. If you want. Speaking of songs, if you want a truly chilling experience, go to Lyrics.com and search for the word "manatee." When I checked, there were twenty-eight entries ranging from the mysterious "I'm not a manatee/Just leave me alone" to the creepy "He made sweet love to a manatee" to the semipornographic (and cringeworthy) "thick and juicy booty like a manatee." There's also one about a space manatee, but I lack the courage to read it.

What (and How) Manatees Eat

Manatees and dugongs are unique among marine mammals: they are herbivores, feeding primarily on seagrasses. No other sea mammal has figured out how to take advantage of these vast underwater meadows.

They have been observed eating more than sixty types of vegetation, including leaves, lawn grass, overhanging branches, and even algae. Manatees have cosmopolitan tastes, eating a wide variety of submerged, emergent, floating, and shoreline vegetation. Some have been seen snatching fish from nets, but this is not a common practice. They can move their prehensile lips (each side of which can operate separately) to select the choicest parts of their dinner on one side and discard the unwanted remainder with the other.

In ordinary times, the mainstay of the manatee diet is seagrass. By the way, seagrass isn't the same thing as seaweed. Seaweed is a form of "macroalgae," coming in red, brown, and green varieties. It's supposed to be good for you. Seagrasses are not grasses, either, though. They are flowering plants more closely related to lilies.

The origin of seagrass is a bit mysterious, for the fossil record is shaky. Researchers believe they stem (yes, a pun) from four different terrestrial lineages, showing the amazing capacity of plants to evolve in the most difficult of environments like brackish water. It seems that vast, shallow water habitats were created by plate tectonics, and the seagrasses and manatees moved right in. The same thing happened in the north Pacific, with kelp emerging in that cooler environment. It seems apparent that manatees and seagrass evolved together in a delicate dance of survival. If the seagrass goes, it seems very likely that the manatees will go as well. And seagrass is in serious trouble, as we'll see.

In Sierra Leone, West African manatees are considered a pest since they swim into the rice paddies and eat everything they can find there. They also have been known to eat clams.

One variety of seagrass is also edible for people: tape grass. Well, you don't eat the grass per se, but rather its large seeds, which supposedly taste like chestnuts.

Seagrasses cover about 2.2 million acres of coastal waters. They work not only to feed manatees but also to serve as a nursery and habitat for fishes, shellfish, and crustaceans. A mere 2.5 acres of healthy seagrass can support one hundred thousand fish and one hundred million invertebrates. Seagrasses also stabilize the lagoon floor with their roots and rhizomes and maintain water clarity by trapping fine particles and sediments with their leaves.

Seagrasses are excellent carbon dioxide "sinks," outdoing even the Amazon Rainforest. They capture carbon dioxide and store it for hundreds or even thousands of years. Here's why. The more slowly vegetation decomposes, the longer it will serve as a storage unit. Decomposition works quickly in the Amazon, with fallen leaves decaying and decomposing within a year or so. Seagrass, which grows in a low-oxygen environment, decomposes slowly, locking up carbon for a lot longer. Among varieties of seagrass, species with thicker stems and leaves hold carbon the longest.

Seagrasses are the only flowering plants to grow in marine environments, although their inconspicuous blooms will probably never grace your mantelpiece. They produce a special kind of pollen designed for underwater propagation, and the neutrally buoyant seeds can travel for miles before settling into mud. Like manatees, they evolved from terrestrial organisms, recolonizing the ocean between seventy and one hundred million years ago. There are about fifty-two varieties worldwide, seven of which are found in Florida. These include large grasses like:

- Turtle grass (*Thalassium testudinum*). Of all the seagrasses, turtle grass requires the most light. A healthy crop of turtle grass signals a healthy lagoon.
- Shoal grass (*Halodule wrightii*), the most common seagrass, is a pioneer species. It grows fast and multiplies quickly, stabilizing the sediment below.
- Widgeon grass (*Rupia maritime*). Widgeon grass grows in very shallow water (often less than a foot deep). If you're wondering, a widgeon is a duck.
- The highly favored eponymous manatee grass (*Syringodium filiforme*).

Smaller species include:

- Star grass (*halophila decipiens*). Star grass gets its name from its whorl-like blades, which grow from a single stem and create a starlike pattern.
- Paddle grass (*Halophila engelmannii*). Paddle grass is the only annual among the bunch. It loses its blades in cold weather, which does the manatees no good whatsoever.
- Johnson's seagrass (*Halophila johnsonii*). In 1980, Johnson's seagrass was named in honor of J. Seward Johnson Sr., founder of Harbor Branch Oceanographic Institute in Fort Pierce, Florida. It seems to be able to thrive under a wide range of disturbing

conditions. Until now, it's been considered a threatened species, found only in southeast Florida; in fact, it has the smallest geographic distribution of any seagrass in the world. However, things are always changing in science. In 2021 the National Marine Fisheries Service proposed reclassifying this grass. Some researchers, based on newly obtained genetic data, charge that Johnson's seagrass is not a unique taxon after all, but a clone of an Indo-Pacific species, *Halophila ovalis*. It was suggested that all individuals in the area were genetically identical, deriving from a single, female plant. There don't seem to be any boys at all. So it's not an endangered species after all. The official name was changed on May 16, 2022. This is bad news for the late Mr. Johnson. Renaming this species also officially removes it from the endangered species list. All is not lost, however, since the South Atlantic Fisheries Management Council has designated all seagrasses as "essential fish habitat" as well as "habitat areas of particular concern." So all seagrasses in Florida retain federal protection. So far.

Manatees also eat marine algae and sea clover, mangrove leaves, and about sixty other plants. Healthy seagrass meadows are considered some of the more productive ecosystems in the world, but among mammals, only the manatee has had enough sense to take advantage of this salad bar. During the last decade, there has been a major die-off of seagrass in the Indian River Lagoon, with a loss of about 90 percent of the seagrass. In previous die-offs, the grass rebounded, but that is not happening now, a matter of existential importance to manatees, fish, and the general health of the estuary. What used to be the crown jewel of the Treasure Coast has become a manatee graveyard. (In May 2022, a ray of hope began to shine when observers saw some seagrasses beginning to regrow in small areas of the Indian River Lagoon. We can only hope it continues; however, even in the best scenarios, it will not regrow in sufficient amounts to tide the manatees over another winter.)

In fresh water, where seagrasses do not thrive, manatees will consume Florida native eel or tape grass (*Vallisneria americana Michaux*), a light green plant whose leaves float along the surface of the water. They also eat horsetail paspalum (*Paspalum fluitan*), another native annual plant.

However, manatees are not picky. They also devour invasive plants such as musk grass (*Chara spp.*), hydrilla (*Hydrilla verticillate*), water hyacinth (*Eichornia crassipes*), and water lettuce (*Pistia stratiotes*), which was introduced to Florida in 1675 from South America. It's been clogging up the water ever since, although continual and rigorous efforts are keeping it in check. On the other hand, research conducted at Blue Spring State Park found that manatees ignored potentially toxic plants like spatterdock, blue-green algae, and water pennywort.

Once, a visitor to the Manatee Observation and Education Center asked me, "Well, what happened to it? Was there a fire?" when I mentioned that much of the seagrass in the Indian River Lagoon had been lost.

Manatees do everyone a good turn by consuming these noxious weeds. They seem to be followers of the "if you plant it, they will come" school of thought. Some researchers believe that all these invasive plants have actually contributed to manatee population growth. It's like an all-you-can-eat salad bar.

Manatees seem to have preferences among the kinds of grasses available. Eelgrass seems to be a great favorite, preferable to the exotic and invasive water hyacinth, which at one time clogged up 120,000 acres of navigable rivers and lakes. In a way, this preference is unfortunate, because for a while during the 1960s it seemed as if manatees were the perfect tool to chomp up and clean out the water hyacinth and hydrilla, another noxious submerged exotic weed with tendrils that can extend more than thirty-five feet. Today hydrilla covers more than 140,000 acres of water in Florida, and manatees are good natured enough to eat as much of the stuff as they can stomach.

Sadly, the 1960s experiment didn't work out. There aren't enough manatees to do the job effectively, and it's been discovered that certain waterbirds like coots are much better at it. Besides, you can't truck two-thousand-pound manatees willy-nilly from one weed-infested site to another, dumping them, and picking them up later. Even if you could, manatees are a protected species. So you can't.

In a similar doomed experiment in Panama, ten manatees were herded into a lagoon to gobble up the dense vegetation that was supporting a booming mosquito population. The theory was simple: the manatees would devour the plants where the mosquito larvae lived, the mosquitoes would disappear, and the manatees could then be released. Five of the manatees escaped the enclosure right away (they are better escape artists than you might imagine). The other five did their best for two years, devouring the weeds at a good clip. It turns out, however, that tropical vegetation can outpace even a manatee's vast appetite. It's been estimated that it would take at least a thousand manatees to control the plant growth in a seven-acre lagoon, and it would be hard to squeeze in that many manatees, even if you could find enough of them to round up.

As much as human beings struggle to find a "use" for every animal on earth, some creatures must be enjoyed for what they are. Manatees earn their place in the world just by being cute and weird. We should require nothing more of them.

Still, manatees do us all a favor with their relentless munching. Despite complaints from some misguided fishermen, the regular cropping of seagrass is beneficial to lagoons, bays, and rivers. It keeps the seagrass at optimum length and tenderness to serve as a nursery for sport fish, and manatee-tended seagrass areas are more productive and nutritious than areas from which manatees have strayed. The devouring of the seagrass and consequent pooping of its remains also helps "recycle" nutrients to other parts of the biosphere. It is true that when manatees are forced to huddle in warm-water refuges during cold weather the seagrass can take a heavy hit. However, it returns to normal when the weather warms up and the manatees leave the area until the following year.

If you stick a hydrophone in the water, you can hear manatee cropping the seagrass. The sound has been described as like that of a teenager eating cornflakes.

Manatees can dine anywhere along the water column—and even outside it. Though most of their eating occurs in waters three to sixteen feet deep, some manatees seem to prefer floating vegetation, whereas others favor submerged grasses.

They have somewhat deflected snouts that enable them to eat from the sea floor by pressing the disk of their faces flat on the bottom and scarfing up the food. Manatees spend the better part of each day devouring not only floating vegetation, but submerged and emergent plants as well. (Emergent plants are those springing up at the water's edge, like sedges and reeds.)

The average manatee meal is low in calories and nutrients, especially protein, so sea cows need to eat a whole lot, just like land cows and horses. It takes approximately seven days for the food to pass through their 150-foot-long digestive systems.

Manatee cousins, the dugongs, are even more adapted to floor feeding and consequently have more highly deflected snouts. You won't ever catch them eating lawn grass. The Florida manatee snout is not as deflected, enabling the sea cows to munch on food all up and down the water column: even within the genus of manatees, each species has a somewhat different degree of deflection, each angle suited to its particular diet.

Scientists used to think manatees ate only the tender leaves of seagrass, but such is not the case. They eat as much of it as they feel like at any given meal. One scientist studied this and discovered that manatees consumed 80 to 95 percent of the aboveground plant and about 50 to 65 percent of the rhizomes and roots.

The manatee diet is not limited to grass and leaves. These resourceful creatures have been observed eating acorns fallen from oaks, barnacles, tunicates, fish, at least one dead rat, and, at times, even their own feces. Sneer if you will, but many other animals share the latter disgusting-to-us habit, including hamsters, guinea pigs, chinchillas, squirrels, dogs, rabbits, hedgehogs, gorillas, orangutans, chimps, and naked mole-rats. This is called opportunistic feeding—chomp down on whatever happens to be around. You never know when you are going to need it. Animals like koalas, who stubbornly refuse to eat anything but eucalyptus leaves, have a hard time of it (in addition to smelling like cough drops all the time).

It's hard to come up with a perfect diet for captive manatees (one reason there are not many of them). Most aquaria provide romaine lettuce and elephant vitamins.

Unfortunately, sometimes manatees must choose between eating and staying warm. The waters of Blue Spring State Park provide a constant temperature, even in the coldest weather, and manatee love to bask there in winter. However, Blue Spring often has no food for them, so typically manatees head out in late afternoon, when it's warmest, to forage for food. But if the cold weather persists day after day, manatees choose to fast rather than risk the cold. They have been known to go a week without eating if the temperature demands it. Unfortunately, this makes things even worse. Normally when a manatee eats, the bacteria in the gut chomp away busily, breaking down the cellulose in the manatee's food and, as mentioned earlier, creating heat to help keep the manatee warm. If the manatee isn't eating, that can't occur, and the manatees can suffer even more.

Manatees can swim surprisingly fast. Although generally cruising at around five miles an hour, they can quadruple that speed for short distances. Source: *Keith Ramos, USFWS ROYALTY FREE (PIXNIO-29320-3000x2008)*

One physical feature that reminds us that manatees are related to elephants is their prehensile upper lip—the manatee equivalent of a trunk, which it uses to grasp and pull food into its mouth. When a manatee approaches food, muscles around the snout flatten and expand into what biologist Chris Marshall has described as a "flare response." The manatee's specialized sensory bristles around the snout help it select the most desirable food items and even help manipulate them into their mouths. They have about eighty bristles on the top lips and half that number on the bottom. But who's counting? Manatee whiskers have been referred to as cutlery (or fingers).

When manatees aren't sleeping, they're usually eating or looking for somewhere to eat. They eat around the clock, making no distinction between brunch and midnight snacks. They often return to their favored feeding grounds year after year, and evidence suggests that mother manatees introduce their babies to those same spots, continuing the family tradition.

Manatees seem to eat a lot: adults consume between 7 and 15 percent of their body weight every day, and calves and juveniles eat even more. This can prove to be a problem in winter refuges where large numbers of manatees gather. These areas are often devoid of seagrass, simply because the water is too warm to support it. Not to mention the fact that hungry manatees would eat it all up the moment it appeared anyway. And although it seems incredible to think that an adult manatee can chow down on a hundred pounds of food a day, a closer look shows us it's not really that impressive. Their metabolic rate is so low that a normal mammal that size would be eating a lot more—like 85 percent more.

Even in their regular dining spots, manatees can devour a vast portion of the lush underwater meadows. Their munching doesn't harm the vegetation; manatees fertilize those same areas with their abundant feces, enriching the aquatic ecosystem in a natural way.

The issue of dining involves a bit of a linguistic push and pull. What word do scientists use to describe a manatee's feeding style? It depends on the scientist. "Grazing" may seem appropriate; however, it turns out that "grazers" are grass eaters, technically, and some researchers refuse to apply it to manatee munching. (The word "graze" is derived from the Old English word *graes*, which does in fact mean "grass.") And seagrasses, the manatee's primary food source, are not truly grasses. They are more closely related to lilies and ginger. (Nonetheless, manatees have been caught nibbling actual lawn grass, if it grows close enough to their waters. I maintain the objection to the word "graze" is a mere quibble.)

Other researchers use the term "browsing," which means to eat the leaves or twigs of woody plants. Similar objections are raised about referring to manatees as browsers. Still, I have seen manatees reach out of the water to snag and sample mangrove leaves. That makes them browsers as far as I am concerned. As well as grazers, since they will eat lawn grass when they can reach it.

That leaves us with "croppers," a more general term that refers to how (as opposed to what) manatees eat. "Cropping" means chopping off the part of the plant above the root. Manatees do that, but they will also "excavate," digging for the rhizomes, which are higher in nutrition. This behavior is more likely to occur in winter. Thus, in the broadest sense, manatees are grazers and browsers and croppers and excavators. There seems to be no end to their abilities. As far as speed eating goes, manatees can chomp down at a pretty good clip, taking about two bites per second.

Each side of the manatee lip can move independently. Like their fellow sirenians, manatees have a rigid, horny grinding or crushing plate on both upper and lower jaws in front of the teeth (but behind the lips), that helps to mash the tough vegetation that makes up most of their diet.

Manatee taste buds are located at the back of the tongue. Manatees have fewer taste buds than most land animals—but more than most other marine mammals. In case you're wondering (and even if you are not), the average manatee boasts 11,534 taste buds (although some had as few as 2711 to as many 23,237 tastebuds), with a few spare ones on the soft palate and epiglottis. Many thanks to researchers Meghan L. B. Barboza and Iskande V. Larkin, reporting in *Marine Mammal Science*, for counting all those taste buds.

There is an idea that manatee tastebuds do more than taste. They may act as receptors for chemical cues from the environment as well as for savoring their dinner, but no one knows for sure. It's also been suggested that manatees use taste to determine the salinity gradients, to detect toxins in the water, and to explore social interactions.

Let's talk teeth. Manatee teeth are low crowned (brachyodont) and possess two rows of large, rounded cusps. Manatees have no front teeth, only molars, which, along with the grinding plates, do the tough but necessary job of grinding up the fibrous seagrasses into tiny bits, so as (presumably) to suck out every last nutrient. This is an important task shared by other hindgut digestors like horses and elephants. For ruminants like cattle, the teeth are much less important. They let their various stomachs do much of the work.

The teeth break down the dinner mechanically and release the inner content of the plants to be absorbed directly (unfermented) into the alimentary canal. However, grass is tough, fibrous, and abrasive, causing a great deal of wear on those chompers. Plants as a rule are high in fiber, although it's worth noting that water plants are generally somewhat less fibrous than their terrestrial counterparts, presumably because water plants don't need to rely on such a rigid cell wall structure. However, even though seagrass is less abrasive than silica-loaded terrestrial grass, the manatee diet inadvertently includes sand, snails, and other abrasive material, necessitating expert chewing and resulting in a lot of tooth wear. The sea cows still ingest a lot of silica, but it's outside rather than inside the plants.

> It takes more than 350 genes to develop a tooth, and it seems to be a devilishly complex process. According to Marianna Bei in her inimitable "Molecular Genetics of Tooth Development," "Teeth, like all epithelial appendages, form via a sequential and reciprocal series of inductive signals transmitted between the epithelium and neural crest derived mesenchyme." Chew on that for a while.

Manatees don't seem to have a specified number of teeth; let's just say they have more than elephants (4) and fewer than catfish (9,280). Manatees have arrived at a sensible if inconsistent medium of between twenty-four and thirty-two teeth. The variable number results from the fact that manatee teeth are constantly on the move! The name for this unusual arrangement is "marching molars," and they are among the many anatomical achievements for which manatees are (or should be) celebrated. Manatees developed marching molars to solve the "tough plant" problem mentioned earlier.

These marching molars progress from the rear of the jaws and move forward. As older, worn-down teeth reach the front of the mouth, the roots are resorbed and the teeth drop out at the front of the mouth, just as if they were on a conveyer belt. As manatee teeth become worn out from crunching on abrasive sand and silica-encrusted plants, they are replaced by new ones (with brand-new grinding edges). It appears that when the teeth come together during the chewing process, the pressure works to force the tooth row forward. This doesn't happen very quickly, though—only about a millimeter a month. (The molars don't start marching until a calf switches from a milk- to a plant-based diet.)

Elephants have marching molars, as well, but with serious limitations. Each elephant gets only six sets. They have only four teeth at any one time: two up and two down. When the elephant runs out of teeth, it will starve to death. (Out of teeth, out of luck.) Not the manatee. Its teeth are continually replaced throughout its long life. The only other animal possessing this unique feature is the kangaroo, in a case of convergent evolution. Because manatee teeth are continually replaced, they cannot be used to "age" the animal, as is often done with other species. (Currently, as mentioned earlier, the only feasible way

This spiffy apparatus is peculiar only to the three manatee species; dugongs are stuck with an outmoded system involving tusks, which is simply not as efficient.

to "age" a manatee is to extract the ear bones from the head of a dead manatee and count its rings.)

In addition to the aforementioned movable chompers, manatees produce a whole lot of saliva as they chew (manatees have impressively large salivary glands), which of course lubricates their meal and helps ease it down the alimentary canal. It appears that calves chew faster than adults, but because their mouths are smaller, with smaller grinding surfaces, they need to chew many more times to ingest the same amount of food. Manatees average slightly more than one chew per second, by the way, when feeding on invasive water hyacinth and hydrilla. However, they take a lot more chews per unit of time with native eelgrass (*Vallisneria*) and thalassia. Scientists discovered all this by sticking hydrophones in the water and just listening. It's not quite clear what all this means, but the authors of one study remarked that since Florida manatees live at the very extremes of where they *can* live, their remarkable, highly dexterous prehensile vibrissae (whiskers) are important aids in the efficient ingestion of food.

> Whenever I consider spit, I can't help being reminded of Amanda Wingfield in Tennessee Williams's *The Glass Menagerie*. At the dinner table, she admonishes her son Tom: "And chew—chew! Animals have secretions in their stomachs which enable them to digest food without mastication, but human beings are supposed to chew their food without swallowing it down. . . . So chew your food and give your salivary glands a chance to function!" Actually, Mrs. Wingfield is wrong. People have secretions in their tummies and most mammals have salivary glands. Even ticks have salivary glands. I'm not sure if you want to know that or not.

Let's continue our trip down the alimentary canal (perhaps not as scenic as the Panama or even the Erie Canal). Manatees possess a bunch of unusual structures in their large digestive tract, which, considered together, exist in no other species. Even if you consider them separately, they are very rare.

Take the cardiac gland, a rare "digestive accessory" organ found prominently in only a few other mammals: the dugong (the manatee's close cousin), the beaver, the koala, the pangolin, the wombat, and the grasshopper mouse. A strange and mostly unrelated collection of creatures. Despite its name, the cardiac gland is not in the heart; it's part of the digestive system, a large structure on one side of the single-chambered, muscular stomach, aligned vaguely in the direction of the heart. Just another way anatomists try to confuse people.

Scientists have long puzzled over the purpose of the cardiac gland; it appears that it secretes hydrochloric acid, pepsin, and mucus and contains enzyme-producing cells to help deal with the dirt and sand manatees inevitably ingest with their diet. It also may produce extra lubrication (mucus) to help in the digestive process by coating swallowed food. The other animals possessing this gland also eat a lot of roughage, either fibrous plant material or, in the case of the grasshopper mouse and pangolin, insects, which have extremely rough "skin" or exoskeletons. A lot of chewing goes on when consuming grasshoppers. Still, one can't help but think that this doesn't explain everything. There are lots of roughage-eating animals out there with no cardiac gland.

The manatee stomach functions mainly to absorb water, leaving the bulk of the real digestive work to other organs down the line. Look in a manatee's tummy sometime and you'll notice how dry it is in there.

Unfortunately, more than just food has been found in manatee tummies. Plastic bags, rope, twine, wire, paper, synthetic sponges, rubber bands, fishhooks, women's stockings, and all the other sad detritus of modern human "civilization" has found its way there as well.

After the food leaves the stomach, it descends to the upper small intestine (duodenum). Manatees and other sirenians have a long, narrow colon as well as duodenal diverticulae (pouches in the intestinal wall). Their presence increases the surface area of the duodenum, which allows a lot of food to pass from the stomach to the duodenum quickly. (At any rate, duodenal diverticulae are an abnormality in people, but perfectly fine in manatees.) The possession of these three odd digestive features collectively separates sirenians from all other animals.

From the duodenum, food travels along the relatively narrow, sixty-five-foot small intestine (that's correct—sixty-five feet). Indeed, the manatee gastrointestinal system is a weighty machine; the entire tract, along with its contents, can compose up to 23 percent of the entire animal's weight, as much as 330 pounds. (I've been told it also has a strong ammonia smell.) Unlike other mammals, manatees and dugongs lack absorptive cells in their small intestine; absorption takes place in the large intestine.

The large intestine or colon, which is also about sixty-five feet long, is where the real gut work occurs. Operations begin with the cecum, a pouch near the top of the colon that collects undigested food from the small intestine and goes to work on it. When you're a manatee, you need every bit of nourishment you can squeeze out of seagrass. The large intestine is laden with helpful anaerobic bacteria and other microorganisms that break down and ferment the cellulose in the plant-based meal. Their own little distillery, so to speak. This process is called, reasonably enough, cellulolysis, a devilish word to say, let alone spell. My spellchecker is having a problem with it.

One thing that makes the manatee colon different from that of the large nonruminants (like the horse) is their crypts of Lieberkuhn. Apparently, they are shorter in the colon than in small intestine, which is the reverse of other nonruminants. I wouldn't mention this at all, except to note that *The Crypts of Lieberkuhn* would make a great title for a horror novel. It sounds very creepy and mysterious, but all they do is secrete intestinal juice. That's because we know a lot about horse digestion. In any case, as mentioned, it takes about a

Not technically part of the digestive system, I suppose, are the manatee anal glands. These glands are located at the recto-anal junction and are large and diffuse, found in clusters on either side of the anal tract within the muscle. Just like the anal glands of dogs, they probably play a role in communication and reproduction. The secretions produced by anal glands are full of protein, mucus, and lipids (fat). Megan Bill and her associates, who studied these glands, suggested they might cause health problems such as a fistula or even tumors, as is the case in dogs and cats. However, it is not clear if this is really the case, and I was unable to find out anything more about it.

week for food to move from the molars through the back end, along with methane gas, a product that proves useful in keeping the animal afloat.

All this lower alimentary canal work is why sea cows are classed as hindgut fermenting digesters, unlike real cows (but like horses and elephants). The stomach really doesn't do a lot of work here. I could add that the manatee digestive system has a lot in common with that of wombats, but I doubt that would explain much. Hindgut digesting is pretty efficient compared to ruminant-style eating, which is why manatees can survive on poor-quality food like seagrass. Any self-respecting ruminant would probably starve to death. It takes between six and ten days for a manatee to completely digest a meal, and scientists suspect this slow process is a great aid in extracting every last bit of nutrition from the seagrass.

At the end of the alimentary canal, manatees produce their famous farts. In fact, farting is rather a manatee strong point and may be of minor help in staying afloat, as previously noted. (People tend to make too much of this.) And of course, at the end of the process (literally), manatees, like the rest of us, poop. Manatee poop is a lot like horse poop—a lovely golden-brown color. Technically, it's called a "bolus" and is about the size of something a Labrador retriever might produce. It's chock full of seagrass remains along with microplastics and parasitic worms. It floats gently on the surface of the water and smells like hay. Sort of.

On May 31, 2017, a mile-long trail of manatee poop forced a beach closure at Humiston Park Beach in Vero Beach. Local health officials did a feel and smell test and reported their findings to Florida Fish and Wildlife Conservation Commission, which calmly told them it was just manatee poop. Workers scooped the poop and the beach reopened the following afternoon. Everyone was relieved, so to speak, but the truth is that human poop is a lot more lethal to manatees than the other way around.

Like the rest of us, manatees can be infested with gut parasites. An ascarid nematode (*Heterocheilus tunicatus*) embeds itself headfirst by the thousands into the stomach mucosa; it also lives in the small intestine. The small intestine hosts another tiny fluke called *Moniligerum blairi*. People got very excited about this organism—it represented a new genus when it was discovered in 1988, so seemingly unique to manatees. Another fluke, the paramphistome fluke (*Chiorchis fabaceus*), prefers the colon as a dwelling place. They can occur in large enough numbers to block the whole intestine.

How Manatees Interact and Behave (Generally Quite Well)

Some animals are nocturnal, like opossums, sneaking around at night. Others are diurnal, like squirrels, running around in daylight. Still others are crepuscular, like deer, preferring the muted light of dawn and dusk. And then there are manatees. They do whatever the heck they want, whenever they like. Time (and time of day) apparently means nothing to them. These quixotic animals can be observed carrying out their regular activities at any time of the day or night. This is especially true during the warmest seasons of the year. In the winter, they tend to gather in the late afternoon to feed and perhaps gossip. They also tend to rest more in the cold weather.

Manatees break up their day into four delightful parts: resting (20–25 percent of their time), eating (20–25 percent), playing (10–15 percent), and traveling (30–45 percent). These numbers are very rough and change by temperature, season, and other factors. One thing is certain: the percentage of time they spend fighting and being disagreeable is 0.

Some scientists have chalked up this lack of scheduling to the fact that manatee brains appear to lack a pineal gland, which regulates this sort of behavior by producing and regulating certain hormones, including melatonin. (They are in good company in this regard with some other marine mammals, hagfish, and mole-rats.) Nearly every other vertebrate has a pineal gland. Walruses and polar bears have really *big* pineal glands.

At any rate, manatees decided to skip the pineal gland and do not seem to have suffered as a result. The French philosopher René Descartes thought that the pineal gland was "the seat of the soul," thus implying that manatees are soulless. However, it is patently obvious that manatees have a great deal more soul than Descartes, who got away with torturing animals by claiming they could not feel pain.

Manatees are classed as "semi-social," and although they seem to get along well with each other and even make special friends, they do not, as a rule, form permanent social-familial bonds like dolphins and in general are considered to have a less complex social life. However, it turns out that the more we know about manatees, the more social they seem. And the more intelligent.

Although manatees often communicate by touch, they also vocalize. Dr. Beth Brady has identified five different call types among sea cows. Source: Rathbun Galen, USFWS ROYALTY FREE (PIXNIO-29366-4015x2700)

Manatees spend a good portion of their time playing and socializing with other individuals. They can be observed kissing (muzzle to muzzle) and mouthing one another. A lot of this kissing occurs at the surface of the water, where it can be viewed by one and all. Play can also be quite active and includes tail thrashing, body surfing, spy hopping (vertically poking their heads out of the water), and a lot of physical contact. They also enjoy bodysurfing, a comparatively new activity in the world of manatees, as it usually involves hanging around one of Florida's countless flood dams. When the gates partially open, the manatees take playful advantage of the strong currents and propel themselves into the torrent. Sometimes they cut back and forth among the currents, apparently enjoying the "rush." At other times they arrange themselves in line with each other but perpendicular to the current. They frequently chat among themselves while playing. They also seem to enjoy a good game of follow-the-leader. With this activity, several manatees arrange themselves single file, and as with human synchronized swimming, they move, breathe, and dive in a coordinated way (but without the spangly costumes). This complicated set of motions indicates that manatees have a good way of communicating with each other, but exactly what that method is, is still murky. The role of leader is a temporary one, as the democratically minded sea cows take turns in assuming this role.

The games go on and on—in fact, manatees have been known to bodysurf for hours. In between sessions, they frequently nuzzle each other or float lazily downstream. Manatee specialists use the word "cavorting" to describe play behavior among the sea cows. For such staid-looking creatures, it is amazing how often they play and how deeply they seem to enjoy it. Manatees of both sexes and all ages get involved, but most cavorting conglomerations include at least some males. Most cavorting occurs during the warm season, when it's safer to expend energy. There's a lot of rolling and jumping around and touching of muzzles and bristles, and manatees clasp each other playfully and tenderly. Play activity can last for hours. Young calves sometimes even are tempted away from their mother's side to join in the roughhousing, but often return to mama if things get a bit out of hand (or flipper). Researchers speculate that all this is a prelude to or practice for mating, but it's much nicer to think they are just having some innocent fun.

Alone or in groups, manatees enjoy investigating new and strange objects. I once worked as a marine mammal observer during a boat race. The entire event had to be postponed for several hours when some manatees swam into the racecourse and took their own good time checking out the buoys and other new markers. Because they are a protected species, it's illegal to harass them in order to get them to move. Only once they were satisfied with the state of affairs did the manatees swim off for a new adventure.

Manatees are known to care for each other deeply. Not only will female manatees who have tragically lost a calf attempt to keep it close to the surface in a vain attempt to get it to breathe, but manatees have long been known to help each other in similar circumstances. I have observed an injured manatee being attended by others who surrounded it and periodically lifted it to the surface so she could get some air.

How Manatees Make More Manatees

Florida manatees, both male and female, reach sexual maturity between the ages of two and a half to nine years, although many researchers think the females mature at the younger end of the scale and males at the older. If a living female whose age is already known gives birth for the first time, we know her age of sexual maturity. Otherwise, scientists must rely on necropsy examination of the ovaries. It's more difficult to determine sexual maturity in males, but scientists measure hormone levels in blood, saliva, urine, feces, and even tears. They also weigh their testes. (Manatees have bigger testes than most mammals their size.)

For the more casual observer, the only way to distinguish males from females is by waiting to see if one rolls over in front of you. There are no external genitalia. In males, the genital slit is close to the navel; in females it is closer to the anus. In addition, females tend to be both heavier and longer than males.

Mating involves one focal female being courted by a group of males called an estrous or mating herd. The scientific name for this mating activity is "scramble polygyny."

Some researchers believe that manatees use taste to determine hormones of receptive females in their environment. Captive manatees also have been observed in mating behavior even while pregnant, an unusual state of affairs for most mammals. We can't be sure if this behavior occurs in the wild. In any case, the usual formation is one female enticing (or evading) a pack of hopeful suitors. The females don't appear particularly interested in this activity and can often be observed trying to escape the crowd of suitors. When really irritated, they may smack their paddles hard against the surface of the water as a warning. In desperation, some even beach themselves to get away. (It doesn't help when concerned humans try to shove her back into the water among the waiting bulls.)

The bulls typically do not fight among themselves for the right to mate. They just hang around the females and try to get closer than their rivals, waiting for the opportune moment. It is true that they can run into each other during this process, but it would be an exaggeration to call this sort of encounter an actual fight. In any case, this nonsense may go on for three weeks or more. When mating is complete, the mating herd breaks up. If the female does not become pregnant during her estrous cycle, she will enter it again during the same year and start dating again. Because of the long gestation cycles, females give birth only every other year or so, and that is under the best conditions. If there is food scarcity or other environmental pressures, she may have a baby only once in a five-year period. If, on the other hand, the mother loses her calf, she is more likely to become pregnant again much sooner, giving birth at the more frequent end of the scale.

Mating itself can occur either under water or on the surface. The loving pair employs a set of postures that may seem more suitable to acrobats than sea cows. Copulation can occur both vertically and horizontally. The pair may face each other during the act, or the male may swim upside down underneath the female.

Manatees have no official "mating season"; however, it does seem true that manatees are more likely to get frisky in the spring, with more calves born in the spring and summer. (Most Amazonian manatees give birth between February and May.) Winter births are rare. This is probably because the summer babies are less likely to freeze to death. (Florida winters can have horrifying cold spells.) Even more important, seagrasses are less nutritious in winter. Manatee mothers need all the nutritional support they can get. And this goes for father manatees as well. Mating drains a lot of energy, and winter mating is even more hazardous to one's health. It can take a long time to recuperate from those endless bouts of scramble polygyny.

How Manatees Mother
(Forget Dad—He's Flown the Coop)

The gestation period for manatees is about thirteen months, with a single calf the usual outcome (about one in a hundred births is of twins). The prospective mom gives birth in a quiet, secluded area, and manatee calves can be born head or tail first. They have been observed pushing their infants to the surface immediately after birth to give them a taste of the vital oxygen they need to survive. (Some researchers believe the calf reaches the surface on its own, but the mother's extreme attention to her baby gives the impression she is helping it. The jury is still out; manatee births are not regularly witnessed.)

The newborn weighs about sixty pounds and is a little more than a yard long. They also possess "fetal folds" of skin around their paddles. Manatee babies are often born dark and tend to lighten as they age.

Manatee moms nurse their babies underwater from a nipple located in the "armpit" (axilla) just behind the flipper. For the record, elephants, which are close relative of manatees, and bats, which are not, also nurse their babies from the same armpit spot. Although calves can start munching seagrass within a few weeks, they don't necessarily stop nursing.

Mother manatees alternate the available teat, switching from left to right. (They close their flipper over the unavailable teat, encouraging the youngster to switch sides.) Each session of nursing lasts about two minutes, once or twice an hour. (Orphaned manatees can learn to drink from a baby's bottle easily—ideally a large one.)

Manatee milk is extremely thick; indeed, it's 20 percent solids. It's higher in fat (13 percent, mostly triglycerides), protein (7 percent) and salt than cows' milk but contains no lactose and only a little bit of citric acid. It does have cholesterol, however. If it becomes

While we are on the topic, we should not forget to mention Manatee Milk, a stout produced by the Slack Tide Brewing Company based in New Jersey. The can depicts a man on a stool milking a manatee from the wrong spot in its anatomy. Oh well, artistic license and all that.

Because they are such attentive mothers, manatees give birth only every three to five years, preferring to spend as much time with each calf as possible before ordering a new one from the local sperm bank.

necessary to rescue and feed a manatee orphan, it's important to get that formula right—emphasis on fat, not carbohydrates, with plenty of short- and medium-chain fatty acids.

Manatee are able to swim when only minutes old and remain close to their mothers, near the teat behind the flipper. (Normally adult manatees swim in single file.) This is probably mainly for protection, but it's also possible that mothers can communicate to their offspring more effectively if they swim side by side. It's also possible that swimming in this fashion produces less "drag," making it easier for the calf to keep up with its mother.

If threatened, mothers position themselves between their calf and the perceived danger, including human swimmers and boats. They will flee if possible, calling to each other the whole while. Most manatee mothers are quite successful at raising their calves, but as in the case with human moms, some show less natural aptitude. Many of these less talented moms do better with later offspring, although some never get the hang of it.

Calves live off their mother's milk for a year or two; usually more experienced moms can wean and free their calves after the first winter. Younger mothers may take two winters, possibly because she is so enchanted with her child that she can't bear to part with it.

Manatees make tender, careful mothers. Calves stay with their moms for up to two years, learning migration routes and where the best seagrass meadows are. Source: *Steve Hillebrand, USFWS ROYALTY FREE (PIXNIO-29302-3504x2336)*

Father manatees are deadbeats and do not participate at all in the serious business of parenting.

Manatee calves tend to nurse for a quite a while longer than strictly necessary. This activity is comforting to both mother and calf. In fact, manatees are not only good mothers—they may be *too* good. First-time manatee moms are often so dedicated to their offspring that they over-nurse them, putting their own welfare at risk. In 2021, a female manatee and her calf were rescued from Blue Springs State Park after observers became concerned about the emaciated appearance of the mother. However, the calf was, according to Missy Gibbs, president of the Friends of Blue Spring State Park, a "butterball." The pair was taken to SeaWorld, where the mother, named Mandy, put on a hefty three hundred pounds. After a four-month rehabilitation stint, both she and her baby, Manilow, were released back near the park waters.

The calves are dependent on their moms not just for food and protection, but for learning lagoon lore: where the best seagrass is and the most efficient routes for getting there. Babies stay close to their mothers for their first year of life, typically within a yard or so, swimming directly behind her flipper-pit (not trailing recklessly behind). Young manatees also seem to take cues from their mothers about how to interact (or not) with people. Shy mothers seem to produce shy youngsters and vice versa. Shyness is the healthiest option for the species as a whole; human beings haven't been a blessing to these animals.

At Three Sisters Springs, part of the Crystal River National Wildlife Refuge, manatees have been observed suckling other mothers' calves and even adopting orphans, a beautiful gesture that seems to put a kink in scientific research. As Helene Marsh remarked rather wistfully in *Ecology and Conservation of the Sirenia*, "If adoption is widespread, the practice will confound estimates of life history parameters, including (1) calf dependency based on the observations of wild individuals, and (2) estimation of annual reproduction using mark-recapture models." I suppose the researchers will have to work around this obstacle somehow. One can hardly wish that manatees would behave less generously.

Currently there are more than a dozen rehabilitation sites, with facilities located not only in Florida, but also in Texas, Ohio, and Puerto Rico. This was necessary because of the huge number of manatees needing rehab services during the Great Starvation event of 2021–2022. There are more than ninety manatees in rehab at the time of this writing due to boat injuries, sickness, cold stress, or simple starvation.

How Manatees Think

All right, all right. Manatees have small brains the size of a grapefruit. A small grapefruit. When we consider the massive size of the sea cow, their small brains seem even smaller. In fact, manatees have just about the smallest brain-to-body-size ratio of all mammals. It's been hypothesized that manatees never needed to develop big brains because they are not predators themselves and have no real predators (except, once again, *us*). Therefore they had no need to become smart. The obvious problem with this line of thinking is that manatees are, in fact, pretty dang smart.

In the first place, size is not everything. There appear to be lots of evolutionary reasons why manatees grew so big. When proto-manatees forsook the land (I've waited my whole life to write the word "forsook") for the sea, they had to develop larger bodies as a heat conservation mechanism. They never had to chase prey around and use their large size alone for protection. "It's not that its brain is relatively small, it's that its body is relatively large," kindly explains manatee scientist Roger Reep.

Cortex folding is also over-rated. The manatee brain is ominously smooth on the outside, quite unlike the rich folding cortexes of humans and dolphins. Early biologists made quite a to-do about all this. One of them, a fellow named Grafton Elliott Smith, wrote in 1902 that the brains of manatees (and their cousins the dugongs) were like nothing more than "the brains of idiots." He described their brains as "extraordinary" and "bizarre."

Smith made quite a career studying brains (and mummies). Of course, one doesn't care to quarrel with Smith, who after all was decorated by the Khedive of Egypt, Abbas Hilmy, with an Insignia of the Third Class of the Imperial Ottoman Order of the Osmaniah. This may be because he maintained (without any proof) that Egypt was the ultimate

It turns out that birds also have smooth brains, and that includes animal wizards like parrots, crows, and ravens. A wrinkled brain may not be as great as we think it is.

source of all human innovation and even civilization. Apparently, he thought that the Aztecs and Mayans could not have possibly come up with the idea of building pyramids on their own.

In any case, Smith was wrong about manatees. They are not idiots, although perhaps their brains may indeed be extraordinary or even bizarre.

Besides, although it is true that higher intelligence has been linked to brains that are furrowed and folded like ours (of course), it turns out that the manatee brain, smooth on the outside (lissencephalic), is pretty complex on the inside. The manatee cerebrum is the largest part of the brain (it is in people as well, by the way). The cerebrum, which includes the cortex, is in charge of general brain function. In manatees, it comprises about 70 percent of the brain. (In humans, it's about 85 percent. Not such a big difference.) Manatee brains also have a well-defined "cortical lamination," which refers to the cellular layers that comprise the neocortex. Just like us. This is complex business. The proof is in the pudding anyway. Manatees appear to be able to learn as much as dolphins can, although they are a lot slower moving and *much* harder to motivate, being by nature rather content with life as it comes and not desperate for lettuce, although they accept treats when offered. Sometimes.

Anatomically, the parts of the brain devoted to visual recognition are small, whereas the parts dedicated to hearing, touching, and using of the mouth and muzzle (proboscis) are well developed.

I suppose I could also mention Rindenkerne, unique cell clusters of sirenian brains that do not exist in other mammals (that we know of). The Rindenkerne seem to control the manatee lip bristles, with some clusters devoted to the thick, long upper lip vibrissae and smaller clusters to the shorter lower lip whiskers. Studies are still ongoing. The connection between manatee brains and whiskers remains a tantalizing mystery.

Perhaps the important thing is to reconsider what we mean by "intelligence." If we restrict our notion of intelligence to the ability to do quadratic equations and compose symphonies, I'm afraid most human beings also would be lacking. However, if we consider intelligence to include the simple ability to get along with others, manatee surpass us every day of the week. (Humans have managed to start a lot of fights *about* manatees—see Craig Pittman's fabulous *Manatee Insanity* for a deeper look. Spoiler alert—it's not the manatees who act insane.)

If one equates intelligence with trainability (not really the same thing, is it?), manatees can definitely be trained to do all sorts of things. It takes a lot to get them interested in doing tricks and climbing into gurneys for blood or urine tests, but they can do it. They're just not crazy about the idea. Playfulness is also a well-known measure of intelligence, and manatees cavort and play throughout their long lives. They also have excellent memories and superb mothering skills.

Believe it or not, it has been difficult to get permission to train manatees. The many regulations designed to protect these highly endangered animals in the wild became an obstacle when working with animals born into captivity or unable to return to the wild because of a serious injury. So far, only the scientists at Mote Marine Laboratory have been granted permission to train manatees for research and "husbandry purposes." Thus, they have been able to develop procedures to work cooperatively with manatees, saving the animals from the stresses that inevitably accompany even routine health checks on other captive sirenians. So the purpose of this kind of training was not directly to measure their intelligence, but to make it easier on everyone to do health checks, such as body measurements, core temperature measurement, voluntary blood collection, voluntary urine collection, and blubber depth measurements. They have learned to breathe in a vacuum-sealed dome on the surface of the water so researchers can learn their metabolic rate and lung capacity. They are also test subjects for various kinds of "critter cameras" so that the behavior of free manatees can be more accurately observed.

The first thing researchers wanted to do was to teach the animals a basic association: in this case between food (the so-called primary reinforcer) and a whistle (the secondary reinforcer). The pupils, Hugh and Buffett, very quickly learned that when they heard a whistle, they would get food.

Each then learned, also quickly, to come to his own "target." Each brother has a separate target: Buffett's target is a white circle with blue trim; Hugh gets a black square with white trim. If they touched their target, they would hear a whistle and then get a treat. This aspect of training is called stationing. All of this is critically important. The long-suffering Hugh and Buffett will wait obediently at their target for up to thirty minutes while the scientists fool around with them. For example, they're trained to offer a pectoral fin for a blood draw and flip 360 degrees for complete body checks. They patiently open their mouth for oral exams, lift their heads, flippers, and fluke to demonstrate mobility, and even swim into a stretcher to be weighed.

We need to get beyond brains when we consider intelligence. Traditionally, we've accorded the moniker of "smart" to animals most like us, without really bothering to define smart. After all, it's been shown that slime molds can figure out the shortest distance between a food item (oat flakes, in this case) a lot better than people can. And if our concept of intelligence is reengineered to include behaviors such as getting along with others and remembering where the heck important resources are, manatees shine. They never forget where their cell phones are. Besides, there's something ethically at stake here. Let's say most people are smarter than most manatees. And let's say Stephen Hawking (or Rembrandt or Beethoven or Shakespeare) was smarter than almost everybody else. It doesn't seem to follow that one's intrinsic worth should be dependent on how well one understands particle physics. If we honored attributes such as peacefulness instead, manatees would rank way above almost every other creature. Including us.

For measurements, Hugh and Buffett are called to their stations. Sometimes they decide to turn belly up, sometimes the other way. In either case, the researchers use a cloth tape to measure their length from snout to paddle and girth at four separate points: axial

Hugh and Buffett have different training whistles. Hugh's is a regular referee's whistle, and Buffett gets a high-pitched dog whistle.

(behind the flipper), umbilicus (the widest part), anal, and peduncal (between the body and the paddle). The blubber depth is measured with a portable ultrasound scanner at various points along their back.

Getting a urine sample is another matter. Although urine chemistry can yield a lot of information, it is really tough to obtain in a male manatee and well-nigh impossible in a lady without sedating or anesthetizing her or "dry-docking" the poor creature, rolling her over and exerting pressure on her bladder, a procedure that is uncomfortable, difficult, and dangerous. But training Hugh and Buffett to voluntarily submit to a safer procedure has been successful. The manatee respond to the command to go "belly up" while floating at their station. One trainer holds a flipper, and another one helps support the manatee by sliding a leg beneath the animal's back. The third trainer presses lightly on the bladder. The researchers then reward the manatee "lavishly" with lots and lots of treats. Over time, Hugh and Buffett have been able to provide urine ever more quickly and with lighter and lighter pressure. The trainers hope that eventually the manatees will respond to the signal to provide urine with no pressure at all.

Hugh and Buffett are making history by giving blood as well. The animals are given a special hand signal that means "roll over and hand me a flipper." The manatee complies and holds still while the flipper is sterilized with alcohol and betadine. A veterinarian inserts a needle into the brachial venous plexus (located between the radius and the ulna), and several vials of blood are drawn. Hugh and Buffett are the first two manatees to donate their blood in this stressless voluntary procedure.

Manatee Health

Manatees are long-lived animals, but it's been difficult to get a good idea of their average life span, partly because so many die from human interference and other external factors long before they have had a chance to live out their natural lives.

Historically, researchers have had to count the incremental growth layer groups (rings) in their ear bones. (Checking the teeth won't work, since manatees are constantly acquiring new ones.) Each growth layer group represents a year, with one layer indicating a period of rapid growth and another of slower growth. (There is some argument about what exactly a growth layer is, but we can leave that aside for now.)

After the death of a manatee, the ear bone is removed, placed in preservative, decalcified, cut into sections, and stained. The method is most accurate for manatees under the age of fifteen. That's because, as manatees age, the ear bones may show signs of resorption, especially in females, mostly because of the inexorable demands of motherhood. Luckily, some individual wild manatees are well known to observers, and we know they can live at least sixty years. The same technique for determining the age of manatees is used for dugongs, toothed whales, pinnipeds, and large ungulates.

For whatever reason, manatees are generally healthy animals. They can fall prey to bacterial infections including pneumonia but deaths from such attacks appear to be rare. Indeed, manatees who have suffered massive wounds from boat propellers have been found idling away their time in sewage outlets and other hideous places without apparent further damage. They can recover from wounds that would fell any other animal. I have seen one with a lung protruding through the skin of the back. A few weeks later the manatee had completely recovered.

The Florida Fish and Wildlife Conservation Commission has an archive of thousands of manatee ear bones salvaged from carcasses beginning in 1987.

A group of manatees is a "herd." They gather to play, graze, mate, or just socialize. Manatee games can go on for hours. Manatees of both sexes and all ages get involved. Although once considered slow-witted, manatees can learn anything dolphins can. However, they are not showoffs and prefer not to perform for public accolade. Source: *Dr. Beth Brady, Mote Marine Laboratory*

Florida manatees, at least some of them (between 30 and 38 percent), have now been documented with a virus dubbed TmPV-1. This condition was first observed back in 1997, when seven captive manatees at Homosassa Springs Wildlife State Park developed warty growths or benign tumors on their lips. This shocked everyone—manatees, with their "super immune systems," had previously been thought to be immune from viral attacks.

Scientists divide a manatee's life into four stages: calves, juveniles, subadults, and adults.

It was also curious and suggestive that this single virus was a type of papillomavirus, the same one that infects human beings. (There are more than a hundred types of this virus, and some of them cause cancer.) As with human papillomavirus, this one is communicable—a sort of "kissing disease" in the eyes of some researchers.

Genome sequencing appears to confirm that this virus evolved right along with the manatee population. It doesn't seem to harm them. Ultimately this research is proving fruitful for humans, especially for cervical cancer. Since this is one virus that manatees can't seem to clear (and we can't, either), studies are underway to figure out what is so special about it. On the other hand, we can't clear chicken pox either, but at least manatees don't need to worry about that.

Three years later, another outbreak occurred in the same captive population. It has not so far been observed in the wild population. Scientists think that viruses can lurk inside the manatee's system

Dr. Greg Bossart, veterinarian, wildlife pathologist, and mammologist, took a sample of the lesion by rubbing disinfectant on them, spraying them with alcohol, then slicing them off with a scalpel. The manatee didn't seem to care. The manatee has "a superbly equipped immune system—so powerful they don't ordinarily die of natural causes; it's usually old age or some human-related cause," Bossart said. "You can almost cut them in two with a motorboat and they'll survive." I rather doubt this, but then again, it's not the kind of thing one actually wants to prove.

and make an outward appearance only when its immune system is sufficiently weakened by trauma or other disease.

It also appears than manatees can run afoul of a fungus called *Bipolaris hawaiiensis*, which in 2015 somehow got hold of an Antillean manatee calf held captive in Brazil, producing blackish skin lesions. The baby was treated with itraconazole for fourteen days and fortunately recovered. One hopes this was an isolated incident, as this is the first time such an infection has been reported in veterinary medicine. In humans, however, the damn fungus can cause subungual hyperkeratosis of the toe, subcutaneous infections, nasal phaeohyphomycosis, invasive and allergic fungal sinusitis, and allergic bronchopulmonary diseases. It also can do rather nasty things to your eyes and on occasion has been responsible for fungal peritonitis and a granulomatous encephalitis. Not something to mess around with. It's not clear to me what exactly is bipolar about this fungus.

Manatees in Danger

Sadly, Florida's largest, most charming, and benign animal resident is under constant attack. The biggest threat to manatees is human activity, such as by hunting (now illegal, but historically present), boat strikes, foreign body ingestion, entrapment, or indirectly from pollution and loss of habitat.

The greatest existential threat to manatees in the long run, however, is not boat collisions, as terrible as they are. It is habitat loss or destruction. This can occur through loss of warm-water refuges, but the current threat is the loss of seagrass in the Indian River Lagoon due to pollution and harmful algal blooms. Our beloved sirenians are simply starving to death.

The situation is so dire at the present time that the state of Florida is now considering what was once unthinkable: provisioning them with lettuce and other supplements. There was a lot of fierce debate on the topic, since it's generally been accepted that feeding wild animals does more harm than good in the long run. However, Florida wildlife officials

The Florida Fish and Wildlife Conservation Commission has classified manatee deaths into nine categories: watercraft (direct impact, propeller wounds, crushing, or any combination of the three); crushing or drowning in floodgates or canal locks, "other" human-caused deaths such as "vandalism," entanglement in or ingestion of fishing gear, entrapment in culverts or pipes; perinatal (the unexplained deaths of manatees less than five feet long not known to have been inflicted by human activity; cold stress/malnutrition (the two are frequently found together); "natural deaths" including birth complications, diseases, "accidents," and phenomena like red tide and other harmful algal blooms. The final three categories are "undetermined" (too decomposed); undetermined" (some other reason); and "verified but not recovered" (a dead manatee no one managed to haul in and examine). Obviously, these categories could use a firm editorial hand, especially considering that different printouts categorize the deaths differently.

Mother manatees use sound to communicate with their young. Most of their hearing is directed toward underwater use, but manatees can also hear airborne noise. Scientists believe that sound is transmitted though the fat/oil-filled jaw and carried to the ear bones. Source: *Dr. Beth Brady, Mote Marine Laboratory*

considered this a special case. The manatees are in trouble because of human actions, not through any fault of their own.

Still, some scientists worried that such action could delay fall migration or cause other harmful disruptions in manatee lifestyle. At first the manatees seemed to want no part of the emergency romaine. However, they soon saw the error of their ways and, during a three-month period, chomped up every bit of the 202,000 pounds of lettuce distributed to (or, in the inimitable words of the *New York Times*, "hurled at" them).

The public is to be congratulated for donating $116,000 in aid of the project. The experiment

Boston Celtics co-owner Rob Hale and his wife, Karen, donated $2 million toward protecting the Florida manatees and their habitat during the crisis: $1 million each to the nonprofits Fish & Wildlife Foundation of Florida and Save the Manatee Club. Good for them!

It's a sad fact that because manatees live in warm water, their bodies tend to decompose quickly, making it difficult or impossible in some cases for scientists to determine the cause of death.

The past couple of years have been disastrous for manatees: 1,217 killed between December 2020 and March 31, 2022. In 2021 we lost 1,100 manatees, a record.

seemed to be working, at least for the manatees who managed to get enough of it. Between January 1 and April 1, 2022, the number of manatee deaths fell to 479, down from 612 during the same period the previous year.

However, it's not completely clear the feeding program can take the credit. The winter of 2022 got off to a late start and was comparatively mild. A more thorough analysis of the data will presumably provide the answers.

In addition, most critics believe that authorities waited too long to start feeding the manatees, and there also have been objections raised about both the quantity and quality of food provided. If conditions worsen in the Indian River Lagoon and manatees leave the area for greener pastures, their migration could strain other parts of the ecosystem.

It's also not clear how dumping thousands of pounds of food into the lagoon will affect the water quality. It was agreed that whatever was offered should be a non-native freshwater plant with little chance of becoming invasive in those waters. Harvesting native plants presents a massive logistical nightmare. On the other hand, there was a possibility that the manatee would reject non-native foods, which might have put the whole operation in jeopardy.

The first test site was a Florida Power and Light Cape Canaveral Next Generation Clean Energy Center. Since it takes manatees about a week to digest their food, scientists had to wait about seven days before seeing the all-important feces, indicating that the manatees were in fact eating and digesting the lettuce. This supplemental feeding was a temporary, three-month trial. Scientists are conducting an evaluation of the program. Early results show that although the manatees were eating the lettuce, several deceased manatees appeared to have lettuce in their stomachs. A little bit of lettuce is apparently not enough to keep these giant mammals from starving. However, the death rate was slower in 2022 than in the previous year. Between January and March 2021, 609 manatees died. In 2022 the number was 477. With warmer weather, it was discontinued in hopes that the manatees would look for new feeding grounds.

If the state decides to go with the plan, seasonal rather than year-round feeding would be the method. I should stress that the program would be run by the state. No one wants private citizens standing on the banks of the lagoon lobbing cabbage into the water. (Manatees have strong site fidelity. That means that once you start feeding them or giving them water, you'd better be prepared to come back and do it every day, because they will return for it.)

Another solution has been offered by the nonprofit Sea & Shoreline conservation group. It notes that seagrass, like many terrestrial plants, shed their leaves in the fall and winter. In fact, seagrass can lose (and regrow) up to 80 percent of its biomass annually. The shed seagrass floats to the top of the water. Sea & Shoreline plans to collect this seagrass and transport it to the state park weekly to feed captive manatees in Homosassa Springs Wildlife State Park, which currently provides four daily feedings of romaine and

Homosassa Springs is now amid the Homosassa River Restoration Project, in which strategically placed "grass cages" or manatee exclusion devices (MEDs) protect tender young eelgrass from munching manatees until it is healthy and thriving.

escarole lettuce to resident and rehabilitation manatees. (There are four residents there now: Betsy, Ariel, Hines, and Keeks.) But scientists believe that seagrass has many more calories and nutrients than lettuce. According to Carter Henne, president of Sea & Shoreline, "This is a win/win for everyone. Our seagrass collection efforts will help feed the rescued manatees and transition them better into the wild where they will need to forage for seagrass; it will help offset the park's costly lettuce budget, which is expected to climb as they rehabilitate more manatees, and it removes floating seagrass from our local waterways where it could sink and compromise areas where Sea & Shoreline has successfully restored seagrass meadows." The idea is to harvest the seagrass from a two-hundred-acre seagrass restoration project in Crystal River, Florida.

There are many plans in the works to replant the seagrass; however, that's going at the problem backward. Until the pollution problem in the Indian River Lagoon is solved, any seagrass restoration plan will ultimately fail. In any case, it takes between three and ten years before a seagrass bed reaches maturity.

If only we can do enough to save them—from us. Like our interactions with most other wild animals, human beings seemed bound and determined to help manatees along the road to extinction. Without us in the picture, manatees would live an idyllic life. Though they have no sharp teeth, claws, or venom to protect themselves, they are generally safe from would-be predators. No one wants a meal *that* big. Predatory whales like orcas might be able to nab one, theoretically, but manatee habitat is too shallow for whales to get them. Predation by sharks or alligators is practically unknown; there are just far easier things for them to eat. Alligators select from a menu of things they can get in their mouths in one gulp. And though it is true that a newborn manatee would just fit into this category for the largest gators, they stay too close to their mothers for this to be a feasible meal in almost all cases, especially when we consider the manatee's extremely tough hide. They have been observed nosing up to an in-the-way alligator and bumping it aside firmly. The alligator moves. (Tonnage rules.) Some manatees

It turns out that the southern house mosquito and other *Culex* species, carriers of the West Nile virus, have aimed their proboscises on manatees, along with their other prey like birds and people. Manatee potentially could be affected by the disease, although this has not yet been documented. Other kinds of skeeters like *Aedes* and *Anopheles* also were noted "interacting" with the manatees in Everglades National Park. "Interacting" means biting. All three of these species of mosquito carry encephalitis. As with the case of West Nile, we haven't seen encephalitis in manatees. Yet. Luckily, they seem resistant to most viruses. But one never knows.

even seem to enjoy teasing gators, chasing them around a bit. Gentle but fearless. When a manatee wants to go somewhere, it goes.

In addition, manatees have acute hearing to detect unwanted advances from would-be predators, a tough, thick skin, and a fortified rib cage. They even can work up short bursts of speed for a quick escape.

Manatees behave in a variety of ways toward humans. Some are sensibly shy and flee if a swimmer is nearby, sometimes giving loud alarms to its fellows who may or may not pay attention. Others take the opposite tactic and approach any available human looking for a pet or a handout.

Pollution is of course a major problem for all marine mammals. Toxic chemicals, especially mercury, can seep into the water and accumulate in the fat tissues of their bodies. Unfortunately, this kind of "bioaccumulation" has not been well studied in manatees, although we are aware of the serious effects it has on their fellow charismatic megafauna, the bottlenose dolphin. It appears that during a dolphin's pregnancy, the mother-to-be "off-loads" many of the contaminants onto the first-born fetus/calf, which then dies. The female may emerge from the failed pregnancy in better shape than before, having rid her body of the toxins. However, manatees have one great advantage over dolphins in this regard: their diet. Dolphins are carnivores that take in toxins through their fishy diet. The fish (especially carnivorous fish) have already accumulated the pollutants. Manatees, on the other hand, are herbivores, which means they are ingesting fewer pollutants from the get-go. They are also a lot bigger than dolphins and can presumably tolerate more. Maybe.

Still, researchers suspect that much the same sort of thing may be happening to manatees, although at a lower rate; there are a lot of otherwise unexplained neonatal deaths among the sea cows. In fact, about 20 percent of all deaths are classified as "neonatal." Manatees have extremely rich, fatty milk, which would retain the pollutants and pass them along to the baby. Bull manatees have no way to rid themselves of accumulated toxins and thus are probably more susceptible to

Though not actually predators, invasive armored catfish enjoy chewing shedding manatee skin. (Yes, manatees shed. But not as much as Saint Bernards.) A few manatees seem to enjoy the interaction, but most appear to find it annoying or uncomfortable and try to rid themselves of the pests. Luckily, periods of cold keep the catfish under control. Climate change, however, is making Florida ever more attractive to these tropical pests.

It made the news when some idiot decided to scrape the name of a one-term president through the algae on a manatee's back. Manatees are usually tolerant of rude behavior, but not *that* tolerant. The animal was probably either physically prevented from moving by the perpetrator or suffering cold stress and unable to move away (the crime occurred in January). Though not physically injured, the manatee was undoubtedly disgusted. As was the general public. The Center for Biological Diversity offered a $5,000 reward for information leading to a conviction, but the perpetrator was never formally identified.

pollutants than are the females. (The human population along the Indian River Lagoon seems to have higher-than-desirable mercury levels, too. Perhaps as more people become alarmed about their own health, the sea mammals can reap the side benefits. The desirable level of mercury in the body, by the way, is zero.)

The main culprits include organo-chlorine agricultural pesticides, polycyclic aromatic hydrocarbons gifted to us by oil and gas companies, polychlorinated biphenyls (PCBs; formerly widely used in the electrical industry), and polybrominated biphenyl ethers that show up as flame retardants in clothing, furniture, and carpeting (but not needed in the water, which seldom actually catches fire).

Dangerous chemicals like these can persist for years in the environment and even in animal tissues, causing kidney and liver damage. They seem to attack important macro-molecules such as proteins and lipids. Manatees are at special risk from noxious chemicals not only because of their longevity, low reproductive rate, and late maturity, but also because, like many other marine mammals, they lack the particular gene (PON1) that reduces oxidative damage to lipids and is the main defense against reactive oxygen species.

A ten-year study from researchers at the University of Florida revealed that Monsanto's Roundup, whose active ingredient is glyphosate, a notorious "weed" killer, has been found in the plasma of 55.8 percent of all sampled manatees. Roundup, the world's most widely applied agricultural chemical, is used, first of all, to get rid of noxious aquatic weeds "cheaply," although the ultimate price is incalculable. The half-life of glyphosate in fresh water is about sixty-five days.

Florida's sugar industry also uses vast quantities of Roundup to hasten crop ripening and increase the total recoverable sugar. They spray the pesti-cide directly on the crop during harvest, where it acts as a drying agent. You may wonder why, if Roundup is so deadly, it can be sprayed on a crop. I'm so glad you asked. So-called Roundup Ready plants are engineered to contain a gene from agrobacteria, which immunizes them against the herbicide. So far, I haven't heard any chitchat about doing the same thing with manatees. So far.

> In case you're interested in the details, glyphosate-based herbicides like Roundup target the shikimate pathway enzyme 5-enolpyruvylshikimate-3-phosphate (EPSP) synthase, the functionality of which is required for the survival of plants. Roundup Ready plants carry the gene coding for a glyphosate-insensitive form of this enzyme, obtained from *Agrobacterium* sp. strain CP4. Once incorporated into the plant genome, the gene prod-uct, CP4 EPSP synthase, confers crop resistance to glyphosate. Now you know, and I'm sure you feel much better.

In any case, this is a crisis. Everyone knows America is suffering from a severe sugar shortage. The levels of glyphosate in animal tissues were higher right around sugar harvest time, coincidentally. The same is true of its breakdown product, aminomethylphosphonic acid (AMPA). The manatees come into contact with the stuff as they seek warm fresh-water refuges. And although we often think of pollutants getting into water via seepage, it's been shown that up to 58 percent of its application may be wind-drifted to and from who knows where.

> It also appears that manatees and other water-dwelling wildlife are adversely affected by massive amounts of drugs—prescription and otherwise—that end up in the river, lagoons, and oceans, especially near highly populated areas.

Farmers and government entities aren't the only ones making use of Roundup and its cousins. Ordinary everyday consumers and lawn care companies snatch it off store shelves and pour or spray it on neighborhood lawns, where, sooner or later, the rains wash it into the rivers, lakes, and lagoons. And thus eventually into manatees, dolphins, and the fish people eat. In laboratory animals, this level of glyphosate exposure causes kidney and liver damage. Since its introduction in 1974, the United States has dumped 1.8 million tons of glyphosate into the soil.

These chemicals may also give people cancer. The World Health Organization unanimously determined that glyphosate is "probably carcinogenic to humans," too. Just a thought.

Manatees are also adversely affected by the infamous red tide, more technically known as dinoflagellate microalgae (*karenia brevis*), which occurs mostly along the west coast of Florida. Red tide is bad for many life forms (including people).

For manatees, the main culprits are brevetoxins, produced by *karenia brevis*, which also target dolphins. These brevetoxins can be inhaled as toxic aerosol spray when diatoms break down at the churning ocean-air interface. This can lead to lethal toxic shock.

Brevetoxins can also be swallowed when manatees ingest filter-feeding creatures like sea squirts, which attach themselves to their regular diet, seagrass. These toxins adversely affect nerve channels and damage the immune system. Frighteningly, it has been observed that some manatees who were killed in boat collisions also exhibited the liver damage characteristic of brevetoxin exposure. It's been suggested that manatees thus affected may be more unable to avoid hazards than healthy manatees for reasons we do not yet understand.

Where did the red tide come from? The answer, oddly enough, is in part Africa, specifically the Sahara Desert and its dust storms. The dust particles, rich in iron, float westward until they reach the Gulf of Mexico, where they are deposited by rainfall. The iron from the dust particles combines with phosphorous from geologic formations in the Gulf to create the conditions fueling the algae blooms that produce the brevetoxins. There's a lot more involved in all this (one hypothesis involves ten steps) but I've provided the basics. The persistent African drought increases the amount of dust and makes everything worse. In fact, increasing algal blooms in South America and Africa resulting from similar factors may be increasing sirenian deaths in those regions as well.

Although some people dispute the role of human involvement in red tide events, the fact remains that red tides in Florida are occurring more frequently and over wider areas. It is apparent to many scientists that so-called natural events like red tides are not nearly as natural as they are made out to be.

Even ordinary nontoxic algae can be bad news for manatees and yet another form of pollution. Nutrient runoff from yards, urban areas, septic tanks, and agriculture spills into the water, which causes the algae to burst into spectacular but often dangerous blooms termed "harmful algae blooms" (HABs). Indeed, water pollution was a major culprit in the 2021 manatee die-off, resulting in (at the time of this writing) more than three times the average number of manatee deaths during the first few months of the year. Broward County, for example, had several failures in the sewer systems, which polluted the canals. Pollution can affect manatees directly, of course, but it more commonly kills the seagrass on which these gentle vegetarians depend.

In March 2011, after a heavy rainfall, an unprecedented "superbloom" of mixed macroalgae developed in the Indian River Lagoon. It was regularly remarked that the algae resembled "pea soup." The algae prevented light from penetrating to the bottom of the lagoon where seagrass grows and also led to poor water quality and consequent fish and shellfish kills. The algae were nontoxic but contained chlorophyll in concentrations more than eight times the historical average and remained for seven agonizing months across much of the area, covering more than 130,000 acres.

The bloom peaked and collapsed (finally) when colder weather hit. Adult manatees, including reproducing females, were strongly affected by the resulting seagrass die-off. This event has often been cited as a tipping point that may have permanently impacted the entire lagoon and its denizens. The following year, brown tide (*Aureoumbra lagunensis*) in the northern Indian River Lagoon again hampered growth of the seagrass. During the period between 2009 and 2012, the lagoon lost an estimated 47,000 acres (60 percent) of seagrass between Ponce Inlet in Volusia County and Fort Pierce Inlet in St. Lucie County. That is most of the Indian River Lagoon.

By July 2012, during the superbloom, researchers were presented with an unusual finding. Dead manatees had been showing up in unusually high numbers since March, mostly from the northern and central parts of the lagoon. Most of the victims were adults. But they weren't injured or cold-stressed. Or starving. In fact, they appeared in rather good nutritional condition, apparently managing to survive on some of the macroalgae (mostly *Gracilaria*) that had killed off their seagrass. Inside the mammals, it was a different story: watery gut contents, multiorgan congestion, intestinal hemorrhaging, and wet lungs—almost as if the animals had drowned. The airways were filled with fluid, mucus, or froth. The kidneys and brains showed similar congestion. The mucosa was thickened and floating loose in the intestinal fluid. The intestines showed signs of "blebs," or protrusions from the cell membrane. The intestines also included microscopic lesions.

Scientists were alarmed and stumped. They looked for algal toxins, contaminants, and a variety of other factors. Finally after an eight-year-long investigation, they found the culprit: clostridial infection from the macroalgae diet. The eventual verdict was that the predominant low fiber macroalgal diet plus the macroalgal compounds could have initiated some of the gastrointestinal lesions. It also turns out that macroalgae produce antimicrobial compounds. This sounds like a good thing in general, but all that macroalgae may have negatively impacted the normal intestinal microbiota of manatees with an associated increase in Clostridiales. Clostridia (*Clostridium perfringens, Clostridioides difficile*) are naturally present in the gut microbiome and fecal samples of marine mammals, fish, crustaceans, and mollusks. It's been suggested that the lower amount of fiber in macroalgae may have made the manatee less able to handle the clostridia as usual, producing diarrhea, bloat, dysbiosis (microbial imbalance), and initiating the clostridial infection. This outbreak is just one more environmental stressor putting manatees, already seriously threatened, at ever increased risk.

The manatees seemed, however, to adjust to the macroalgal diet, at least to some extent, restoring the gastrointestinal microbial balance after transitioning to a macroalgal diet. At least there was a decrease in morbidity and mortality cases in the months and years after the peak of what scientists term a UME, or unusual mortality event. We know that other hindgut digesters like horses experience the same thing when their diets were changed.

These single-celled phytoplankton blooms cut off sunlight to the seagrass below. When natural sunlight is restricted for a long period of time by the presence of algae, seagrass leaves become

> Various government entities and local conservation groups regularly attempt to "restore the seagrasses," but most of these efforts meet with little success. You can plant all the seagrasses you like, but if the area in which they are planted is polluted, they will all just up and die again. The only way to save the seagrass is to save the water it grows in.

shorter and narrower and produce fewer leaves per foot. Eventually it can die and deprive manatees of their main source of sustenance. And then the manatees starve to death.

Unfortunately, these HABs are increasing worldwide in nearshore environments—exactly where manatees make their home. In 2013 a "brown tide" of algal bloom (*Aureonumbra lagunensis*) occurred in the Indian River Lagoon, home to a large proportion of Florida's manatees, who are traditionally drawn there by its warm waters and once abundant food supply. The algae itself was not toxic to manatees, but it covered much of the surface of the water and killed off about 60 percent of the vital seagrass below. Deprived of their regular diet, manatees were forced to look elsewhere for dinner; so, as mentioned earlier, many of them were forced to feed on red drift algae (*Gracilaria*), not part of their normal diet. Although some types of algae can be profitably eaten by sirenians, others contain neurotoxins. And some of those toxins can stick to the seagrass that manatees normally eat. Manatees forced to eat algae when no seagrass is available (thanks to the algae bloom) can become sick and die.

Indeed, in the past decade the Indian River Lagoon has lost 90 percent of its available seagrass, thus casting the future of this critical manatee habitat into grave doubt. However, we can be cautiously optimistic.

During the peak spring breeding and calving season, the Indian River Lagoon supports about 70 percent of Florida's East Coast manatee population. It is essential during all seasons. Restoring the lagoon is critical, but it requires political will to do it. "It's been an uphill battle," complained Paul Fafeita in 2021, president of the Clean Water Coalition of Indian River County. "Now the hill is getting steeper." Referring to the water quality, he remarked, "We've got 156 miles of trouble here." That's the length of the whole lagoon.

Many kindhearted, well-meaning folk, either singly or in groups, try to mobilize to feed manatees on their own. Unfortunately, this is generally a bad idea (and it's also

I'm writing this book in 2022, and it's been a disastrous year for our sea cow friends. Indian River Lagoon manatees are starving to death at a rate never before seen, with nearly 10 percent of the population killed. Previous optimism about the manatee population expanding and ensuring its survival into the next hundred years or so has faded. There are plans to "clean up the lagoon" (there are always plans to clean up the lagoon) during the next seven years, but it's pretty clear that the manatees may not have seven years left. In September 2021, Florida allocated another $53 million (with a similar amount to be spent annually) to help the Indian River Lagoon by eliminating the three-thousand-plus septic tanks that line the lagoon and whose contents leak into the water at an alarming rate. Though it is the twenty-first century, a surprising number of Floridians are dependent on septic rather than sewer systems. The state also plans to update three sewage treatment plants, reducing total nitrogen by almost 265,000 pounds a year and phosphorus by nearly 43,000 pounds a year.

illegal). Manatees remember food sources and they return to places where they have been fed. However, since it is extremely unlikely that people would be able or willing to provide a hundred pounds of food each day, every day, for every manatee in need, sooner or later they would stop feeding them, and the manatees would be worse off than before. Manatees do best if they can leave a barren area to forage for food elsewhere, hopefully in waters that are warm enough to support them. Manatees who can find nothing to eat in their usual warm waters may be forced to swim far afield into colder waters where they can suffer cold shock. In too many cases manatees are forced to choose between starving to death and freezing to death. Humans are responsible.

Even rescuing manatees can become a political tug-of-war. Back in 1998, when Jeb Bush was running for governor of Florida, he somehow got mixed up with a frostbitten manatee coincidentally also named Jeb. (It really was a coincidence. The animal was named after a relative of one of the researchers.) The unfortunate mammal (Jeb the manatee in this instance) had frozen a flipper in cold Georgian winter waters) and had been treated at SeaWorld. Jeb the human, possibly smelling a photo op, decided to accompany the manatee on his trip to Blue Spring State Park, where Jeb the manatee was to be released. Jeb the human helped Jeb the manatee by pouring water on his back during the trip. Manatees really don't need to be "watered" like dolphins to keep their skin moist, however. Their elephantlike hide can stand a little drying out. However, the water does help regulate their temperature so that they don't overheat or freeze. (Jeb the manatee was also wrapped in foam.) At any rate, Jeb the manatee, fitted with a tracking device, was hoisted off the truck and into the water with great fanfare. Jeb the human later announced that manatees were his favorite mammal. Jeb the manatee, however, lost his tracker in May 1999. Eventually his carcass was discovered off the coast of Vero

The same is true for boat owners who enjoy squirting hose water into manatees' mouths. Undoubtedly this is a pleasurable activity for the sea cows; unfortunately, it's also an invitation to play in traffic.

Beach in January 2001, right after a cold front. He may have been headed back north to Georgia.

The whole sad incident is just more evidence of manatees' strong "site fidelity," returning year after year to their favorite warm-water haunts, even if that means bypassing nearer, more convenient ones. This is apparently what happened to Jeb. He may have been looking for the one refuge (an industrial plant discharge) with which he was familiar. Or he could have been heading south but not quickly enough during the cold snap. The shallow waters of the Indian River Lagoon get warm—and cold—really fast compared to the deeper ocean.

If you see a starving or sick manatee, the best chance of saving it is to call Florida Fish and Wildlife Conservation Commission for a rescue/intervention at 1-888-404-FWCC (3922) or use VHF channel 16 on your marine radio. And, as you might expect, there a free app (FCC Reporter App) for your phone or tablet.

At any rate, Jeb Bush maintained his love for manatees, at least for a while: "There's an endangered species that's close to being extinct in Florida waters, and I don't want to be part of that," Bush announced at a July 2000 cabinet meeting. However, when push came to shove, the governor's announced adoration for the imperiled mammal did not extend far enough for him to actually do anything to save them. Members attending a summit meeting in October 2000, which convened both environmentalists and representatives from the boating industry, modestly suggested that assessing a $10 fee on each new boat registration would raise enough money to hire one hundred new wildlife officers to patrol manatee areas. Jeb Bush rejected the idea out of hand. "It smells like a tax," he said. As a result, the Save the Manatee Club sued everybody, forcing state and federal agencies to agree to set up new speed zones and refuges. Bush had a fit. "Recognizing the frustration and heavy burden on Florida boaters, I appealed to Gale Norton [secretary of the interior in his brother George's administration] . . . to delay any announcement and possibly forgo implementation of federally designated refuges and sanctuaries." Done. A record

In May 2022, the Save the Manatee Club, the Center for Biological Diversity, and the Defenders of Wildlife teamed up to sue the Environmental Protection Agency in federal court. The suit alleges that the 2009 water quality standards are not being adequately enforced, specifically pointing to the relentless release of pollutants into the Indian River Lagoon from leaky septic tanks, wastewater treatment discharges, fertilizer runoff, and other unwanted nutrients. In June 2022, the government reached a deal, agreeing to update the definition of "critical habitat" for the first time in more than *four decades*. There will be a close look at which Florida waterways are most critical for the survival of the species. The government must now take into consideration such factors as seagrass loss, declining water quality, and loss of warm-water refuges as factors threatening the very existence of sirenians. For the record, the Florida Fish and Wildlife Conservation Commission wanted to do this back in 2010 but said it didn't have the money to undertake more action. Animals with federally protected status are more than twice as likely to reach sustainable levels.

number of Jeb's favorite mammal was killed by boaters that year.

These boating disasters occur all year long and affect manatees of every age. This is probably a massive underestimation, since the carcasses of many salvaged manatees are too decomposed to accurately determine the cause of death. About 30 percent of all manatee deaths are listed as due to boat strikes, which are divided into three classes: propeller wounds, blunt trauma, and a combination of both. Not every collision results in death; an astounding 97 percent of all wild adult manatees bear scars resulting from boat strikes. Necrop-

Scientists still do not know why manatees keep getting hit by boats. They can hear them and apparently can determine where the boats are in relation to themselves. In many cases, it is believed they simply cannot react quickly enough. Or they may be sleeping on the surface of the water. More research is needed.

sies have often shown well-healed rib fractures as well. Reasonably enough, the larger the boat, the more deadly any impact will be. Although manatee rib bones are dense, they are also extremely brittle, more so than other mammals, with a lower "fracture toughness." Scientists are even conducting studies on manatee bones to determine their "energy of fracture." When a rib bone shatters, it can break into hundreds of sharp pieces, piercing the lungs. The results are grotesquely predictable. Deaths from propeller wounds are also substantial but probably account for less than half of boat-related manatee deaths. Victims of boat collisions can be treated with flotation jackets, but it's obviously better to prevent the accident than to have to treat it.

When a manatee's flippers have become entangled in fishing lines, scientists have developed interesting bandaging techniques that include petroleum-jelly-based ointments, porous tape, and superglue.

One risky but unavoidable habit leading to the demise of many a manatee is their diving behavior. Manatees largely feed on submerged seagrasses, which grow in shallow water. A study conducted between 2002 and 2006 (but not published until 2016) quantitively examined the factors that pose the greatest risk. They observed the behavior of nine manatees carrying GPS tags and time-depth recorders in Tampa Bay, Florida. They found, to no one's surprise, that the sea cows were at greatest risk when they were over seagrass, when it was night, and while stopped or moving slowly. (That's practically all the time.) The scientists also found out that manatees were less likely to be hit when they were more than about fifty yards from a charted waterway. I would think this would be common sense, but it's nice to have it all spelled out, I suppose. The methodology was certainly impressive, applying "a Bayesian formulation of generalized linear mixed models to depth data to model the probability (Pt) that manatees would be no deeper than 4 feet from the water's surface as a function of behavioral and habitat covariates." This is the kind of thing science is very good at.

Most collisions are not reported, in any case, either because the boat operator had no idea what was hit or perhaps did not want to go through the trouble of reporting it. (Many accidents occur when manatees are floating on the surface and basking in the sun.) Concerned manatee lovers and environmental activists along with boaters of common sense have advocated for low-speed zones where manatees are likely to be present. Almost always, however, there is some special interest group representing people who think they have a God-given right to go as fast as they want, anywhere they want, who take the issue to court. Even the tiny fraction of water so regulated on behalf of manatees is under continual attack.

Even manatees who aren't killed outright by boats can suffer lifelong health and reproductive consequences after getting whacked by one. Boat traffic can also seriously increase the turbidity of the water and harm the seagrass, which supports fish as well as manatees. Although encasing propellers in propeller guards would reduce wounding, it's not enough. The deadly effect of boat strikes could be largely ameliorated if boaters followed one single tactic: slow down! In almost every instance, collisions occurred when boats were traveling at more than fifteen miles an hour.

In some instances, manatees have become so habituated to friendly human company that they actually seek it out and solicit petting. In the long run, this behavior is harmful, as not all humans have good intentions. For some bizarre reason, manatees have been shortchanged in the protection-from-people department. True, humans are not allowed to poke, prod, kick, chase, hit, or ride them. It is even illegal to touch or feed them. Doing so can get you hit with a $500 fine and up to sixty days in the clinker. That's Florida law. And you don't want to get the feds involved: you can be charged a $50,000 fine and spend a year in prison. It's illegal to go around petting whales, too, but that issue just doesn't come up for some reason. Even well-intentioned people, by petting or feeding manatees, are habituating these wild animals into approaching people—and boats—creating opportunity for cruel people and careless boaters to injure or kill them. There's a saying in the wildlife world: "A fed animal is a dead animal." Truly, the single best thing people can do for manatees and other wild animals is to leave them alone. However, there seems to be no easy way to prevent people from engaging in behavior they find rewarding and harmless aside from enacting stricter regulations.

This brings us to the fraught topic of "swimming with manatees," a hugely popular activity enjoyed by tourists and residents alike. Many conservationists oppose the practice as being disruptive to the natural behavior of manatees. Some manatees enjoy human company, but others are so fearful of people

Aviva Charles and her colleagues researched temperament in sixteen captive manatees along a boldness/shyness continuum. They conducted "novelty tests," using unfamiliar objects, sounds, and even a human stranger. They also relied on records of behavior from the animals' keepers. I should mention that one of the standard items used in tests like this are "aggressive to humans" and "aggressive to conspecifics." Since we're talking about manatees, these criteria were simply eliminated from the study. Manatees just don't exhibit aggression. The scientists suggested that by better understanding the level of "boldness" in manatees undergoing rehab, individualized plans could be drawn up for their release. The scientists also suggested that captive manatees would benefit from more enrichment programs.

that when they encounter swimmers, they leave the area, even if doing so sends them into freezing water where they can suffer or even die. The friendly manatees people encounter on commercial trips are the only ones not afraid of us. Others may have left the area and be suffering. Overly friendly manatees have become so acclimated to people, putting themselves in grave danger from idiots who want to ride, poke, or stab them. It's happened.

Manatees can get crushed in locks or trapped behind levies. In fact, in 2020, 20 percent of manatee rescues were due to the animals getting caught in human structures. Horribly, in December, near Miami's Little River, a manatee was decapitated by doors on a salinity control lock. Eleven manatees were crushed or drowned by floodgates, reversing an earlier trend in which almost none was killed. These accidents are totally preventable; floodgates are supposed to be equipped with manatee sensors that allow them to open when a manatee needs to go through.

Manatees also can become entangled in fishing lines. The lines can get caught around flippers, resulting in amputation. A 2017 study showed that over twenty years, 11 percent of deceased manatees studied had ingested trash or shown signs of entanglement.

And it's not just water-related items that manatees can run afoul of. All kinds of human detritus seem to end up in the water, causing harm to our sea cow friends. One such story, however, has a happy ending. This is the tale of Schwinn, the bicycle-wheel bound manatee. In October 2019, a manatee later nicknamed Schwinn by researchers and Wheelie by concerned manatee watchers somehow managed to get himself completely encircled in a bicycle tire. He was first reported in San Fernandino Beach; he then disappeared but resurfaced a few months later at Blue Spring State Park. Large numbers of would-be rescuers hastened to the scene. Staffers and volunteers from the park, Clearwater Marine Aquarium Research Institute, Florida Fish and Wildlife Conservation Commission, Jacksonville Zoo, Save the Manatee Club, SeaWorld, U.S. Fish and Wildlife Service, and Volusia County were on hand to monitor and try to catch the elusive Schwinn. It proved impossible. Blue Spring is swarming with manatees during the winter season, and Schwinn managed to evade his would-be captors by darting in and out among them. It became too dangerous, including to the other manatees, to effect a safe rescue. He could not be approached by boat, canoe, or even by foot. He then disappeared again, no one knowing where he spent the summer. Certainly no one reported seeing a bicycle tire entangled manatee.

But in December 2020, Cora Bercham, a Save the Manatee Club research volunteer spotted Schwinn on the club's live webcam and reported the sighting immediately to the proper agencies. Miraculously, Schwinn had managed to free himself from the wheel, although it had left deep scars on his body. It was determined that in this case, a boat propeller had sliced through most of the tire, ironically freeing the entrapped creature. Schwinn is currently being monitored; however, given his ability to simply disappear, it may be a daunting task.

Manatee biology alone puts sea cows in danger. Large mammals typically propagate slowly. As mentioned earlier, manatees have a long gestation period and bear only one calf every other year or so. Twins are rare and triplets have not been documented. When calamity strikes in the form of algae blooms, habitat loss, prolonged freezing weather, or disease, manatee mortality can spike sharply up, endangering the species' future.

In 2020, at least 58 percent of all rescued manatee had gotten into trouble because of human activity, primarily boat strikes.

The World Conservation Union lists all sirenian species as endangered, threatened, or vulnerable. The Florida manatee may be in the best shape of the lot, however, partly due to a strong conservation effort by the state, but manatees are continually and increasingly threatened by boats, pollution, and the pressure of human population. A few years ago, in more ruggedly cheerful news, the U.S. Geological Survey and the Florida Fish and Wildlife Research Institute announced that Florida's manatee population is "highly likely to endure for the next 100 years, so long as wildlife managers continue to protect the marine mammals and their habitat." This rosy announcement, however, came just before a massive die-off of manatees that occurred in 2021. This, by the way, is a federal declaration under the Marine Mammal Protection Act (MMPA) originally enacted by Congress in October 1972. This legislation is designed to prevent marine mammal species and populations from diminishing, *as a result of human activities*, beyond the point at which they cease to be important functioning elements of the ecosystems to which they belong.

Unfortunately, "unusual mortality events" are becoming more usual every year. And I don't know what to make of the "next hundred years" bit, which is a tiny slice of time compared to the millions of years that sirenians have graced the earth. On the other hand, it's difficult to be sure that anything or anyone will still be around in a hundred years.

Manatees have been protected from hunting since 1893, one of the first species awarded such treatment. Currently manatees in the United States are protected under federal law by the Marine Mammal Protection Act of 1972 and the Endangered Species Act of 1973. They are also protected by the Florida Manatee Sanctuary Act of 1978. Additionally, the U.S. Fish and Wildlife Service and the Florida Fish and Wildlife Conservation Commission have designated both Federal Manatee Protection Areas and Florida Fish and Wildlife Conservation Commission Protection Zones in an effort to keep them safe from us.

Rescuing a sick or injured manatee is a complex and difficult job. There is always stress involved in the capture, restraint, loading, and unloading of the animal, although it must be said that manatees are able to keep remarkably "cool" during the whole procedure, their stress hormones remaining relatively stable. They don't go nuts like dolphins. Indeed, they maintain a calm and philosophical attitude toward it all. Some protocols specify that manatees should not be sedated during transport. They are already calm enough.

Generally, manatees can handle transports lasting under two hours with aplomb as long as their temperature requirements are met. The space afforded by the container should be wide enough for the flippers, according to most protocols, but not wide enough to allow the manatee to turn around or, God forbid, flip over. It's difficult enough to deal with a manatee right side up. If possible, the container should be in a transverse position on the vehicle; if that isn't possible, then the animal should go in headfirst. Ideally, of course, a veterinarian should accompany the team, but this is not always possible in an emergency situation.

Rescuers are required to monitor the rescued manatee's health in much the same way as I described for a regular health check.

How Many Manatees Are There?

The Florida manatee was once on the edge of extinction. The species manatee was listed as endangered in 1967 under the Endangered Species Preservation Act of 1966. In 1991, only about 1,267 manatees were actually counted. However, thanks to critical protective measures, their numbers have been rebounding, with at last count more than 6,300. That is a minimum number—manatees that were actually counted. Researchers, using clever extrapolation, estimate the true number is about 7,500 hundred at the time of this writing (April 2022).

However, this is an ever-fluctuating number, and it takes only one cold snap, red tide event, or other calamity to reduce their numbers again. Matters were distinctly not helped, when only a few months into office in March 2017, the Trump administration decided to "downlist" manatees from "endangered" to merely "threatened." This boneheaded move occurred despite the fact that no one really knows what a healthy number of manatees actually is: Ten thousand seems much too low. Is one hundred thousand too high?

One thing is for certain, at the time of this writing, Florida manatees—after having "improved" their status—are "dying by droves" according to the Save the Manatee Club. *Don't worry about a thing*, the feds counseled. *Nothing is really going to change. You won't notice a thing*. Nothing except for the four hundred dead manatees that showed up during the winter of 2021. They were actually quite noticeable. For example, in February of that year, the bodies of thirteen manatees were discovered on one of the spoil islands in the Indian River Lagoon, home to about a third of Florida's manatees.

In 2021, we lost a record-setting 1,101 manatees (that we know of). Most of them (58 percent) were not necropsied due to pandemic restrictions, the poor state of the carcasses, or simply the overwhelming numbers of dead manatees. And when we don't know

The Antillean manatee in Puerto Rico is suffering similar threats due to environmental degradation and habitat destruction.

why manatees have died, we are handicapped in planning a future for the species. We do know that about 10 percent of the necropsied deaths were caused by collisions with watercraft. This is undoubtedly a significant undercount. During 2021, 159 manatees were rescued—a huge number compared to other years. Most of the rescued manatees were suffering from starvation (Indian River Lagoon) or red tide poisoning (southwest Florida). A large number were also hit by boats.

Many of the starving manatees were found to be 40 percent of their expected weight. Martin de Wit, a veterinarian who does necropsies (animal autopsies) for Florida Fish and Wildlife Conservation Commission, remarked that this was something never before seen in these large mammals. Some were so gaunt that they were actually concave.

If the present trend continues, we stand to lose more than two thousand manatees in 2022, amounting to a third of the present population—an unsustainable loss. In addition, none of the original conditions that led to the classification of manatees as "endangered" has improved: the water is just as polluted, the human population and number of boats in Florida continue to rise, and manatee habitat is under continual threat due to development. As the crisis deepened, the Florida legislature appropriated $8 million in 2022 to the Florida Fish and Wildlife Conservation Commission. The money will go toward increasing manatee access to warm-water refuges and restoring natural foraging habitat. And for the first time ever, Fish and Wildlife is considering provisioning manatees to help them through a hard winter.

There are some bright spots: for four decades, researchers at the U.S. Geological Survey Manatee Sirenia Project, working cooperatively with state and federal scientists and managers, have been conducting detailed studies on manatee life history, population dynamics, and ecological needs of the West Indian manatee.

To do this, we need to know how many manatees there are, so every year (except for the plague year 2021) the Florida Fish and Wildlife Conservation Commission relies on a synoptic survey to get an estimate. "Synoptic" means to look at something comprehensively and at the same time. Manatees are tricky to count since they tend to dwell in murky water, often overhung with branches or choked with algae, and they don't stay put. They do surface, but often only for brief periods. And when they do, they often blend in with their surroundings. Even if you are close to them, you can mistake them for floating bags of trash. (It's happened.) On the other hand, they can spend twenty minutes under the dark water, where it's very difficult indeed to spot them. Sun glare, water turbidity or choppiness, and cloud cover do not help matters either. To further complicate matters, manatees often find refuge in narrow waterways, areas that are hard to survey.

The Florida Fish and Wildlife Conservation Commission is required by law to submit an annual report to the Florida legislature on the expenditures from the Save the Manatee Trust Fund. The trust fund is the main source of funding for the state's manatee-related research and conservation activities.

Though manatees are impressively large, these gentle creatures are in desperate need of our help if they are going to survive. Source: *Dr. Beth Brady, Mote Marine Laboratory*

Still, one must try. Aerial surveys are the most cost-effective method and are hence the most relied upon. An interagency team conducts a survey one to three times every year between January and March (and have done so nearly every year since 1991), when we suppose all the manatees are "home" and not wandering around Atlantic City or something. All known wintering refuges, including natural springs, deep canals, and areas that receive discharges from power plants or industrial factories are surveyed in accordance with (if you want to know) Florida state statute 379.2431(4)(a). This law requires an annual, impartial, scientific benchmark census of the manatee population. Surveys are taken from sites in Jacksonville to the Keys on the eastern coast and from the Wakulla River to the Everglades on the western coast. The results provide authorities with a *minimum* number of manatees over the area surveyed. "Minimum" because many will escape notice. The most important function of the survey is to give a general idea of the population trend. Even if we miss some manatees, we can easily tell if their numbers are increasing or decreasing. It has been hypothesized that, in order to count the most manatees, you'd better head out early in the morning. After things warm up during the day, many of the "monitorees" leave their warm-water refuges to forage in greener pastures, leaving the observers with a serious undercount.

Counters look for a period of clear, windless skies after a few days of 49 degrees or lower and when surrounding water is below 68 degrees. More manatees are spotted just as it starts to warm up a little, when the manatees tend to rise to the surface and are more visible.

These conditions must prevail in *all* parts of the state to conduct the survey, which counts manatees in the entire state at the same time. Otherwise, the manatees are likely to move from one spot to another and be double-counted. The task is not made easier when we realize that for planning purposes, the survey must be scheduled several days in advance.

Every so often, people (at least some people) are keen to know the carrying capacity of various manatee hangouts. The term "carrying capacity" refers to the number of organisms a given ecosystem can sustain healthily. This would be great to know; unfortunately, it's an extremely difficult number to come by. In the first place, it is still unclear as to what the specific nutritional needs of manatees are. And although measuring the total submerged vegetation in any one place is straightforward, it's quite another matter to determine the quality of it. In addition, external events can cause rapid seagrass die-offs that quickly alter what's available. Besides, manatees are not oysters. They are nomadic and travel with ease from one place to another, sometimes covering hundreds of miles. Everything is made even more complex when we understand that no one knows what the optimum number of manatees actually is. How many manatees lived in Florida a hundred years ago? Or a thousand, when presumably there were not enough human beings around to menace them seriously?

It's also important for manatees to be identified. That's where MIPS comes in: the Manatee Individual Photo-identification System, a program developed and coordinated by the U.S. Geological Survey (USGS) Sirenia Project in collaboration with Florida's Fish and Wildlife Research Institute and Mote Marine Laboratory. So far, the project has collected data on more than five thousand manatees since 1978. The goal of this regionwide program is to model manatee demography rates.

Manatees get injured by boats and propellers and entangled with ropes and fishing gear. Survivors of these encounters incur telltale scars on their backs, heads, or tails, which can be duly recorded, studied, and used for identification. The data is shared among the agencies via encrypted USGS servers. No one wants sensitive or top-secret manatee information to get into the wrong hands.

A future goal is to integrate MIPS data with manatee genetic data. Scientists hope to be able to estimate annual survival rates of calves and subadults as well as to assess the rate of acquisition of new scars in relation to management actions like adding new manatee sanctuaries and regulating boat speeds. Medical researchers are also keen to know the secret of the manatee's impressive wound-healing ability, which is also documented by the MIPS program via its extensive individual image records.

Monitoring Manatees

Manatees are great travelers, but it's only comparatively recently that we have been able to accurately track the movements of at least some of them. (People can't just go around willy-nilly capturing and tagging manatees, though. Permission must be obtained from the U.S. Fish and Wildlife Service.) Even though manatees seem to have been able to look out for themselves all these millions of years, it appears that since we've been systematically destroying their homes and running into them with boats and jet skis, it's now up to us to save them.

In order to be tagged, a manatee must be captured using nets deployed from a specialized "manatee capture/rescue vessel" and staffed by a capture team. The capture crew is made up of people with experience in capturing and handling big marine mammals. This operation can occur either along the shore or in open water. Usually, an aerial observer flying in a single-engine plane locates the target manatees and guides the capture boat in setting the net. Other vessels (the assessment team) wait close by. Their job is to collect data on the capture attempts, carry gear, and provide help when needed.

After capture, the manatee may remain aboard the capture boat or else be transported to shore for a health assessment and tagging. The data gathered provides baseline information on manatee health, reproductive status, and nutritional condition.

As might be expected, there's a lot to check on a manatee. A full-scale exam might include:

- Photo documentation of wounds, lesions, and scars. This is the primary way in which manatees are identified.
- Measurement of length, girth, and weight (morphometrics).
- Measurement of backfat thickness (via ultrasound).
- Respiration check. A good average is about one breath a minute. If the manatee does not meet this standard, the researchers may pour water over the closed nostril to stimulate breathing. They also note whether the breath is deep or shallow and if it is accompanied by an odor.

- Heart rate check. Researchers check the heart rate with a stethoscope or an electrocardiogram monitor. The normal heart rate for an adult manatee is 51 to 66 heartbeats per minute. For a calf, it's 61 to 75 heartbeats per minute.
- Heart health check. The heart is also checked for murmurs, palpitations, trills, and arrhythmias.
- Capillary refill time. This is an excellent measure of the manatee's circulatory health. The researcher places a finger against the pad of the inner lip and checks to see how long it takes for the blanched-out area to return to its normal color. Pale, cyanotic (blue) or icteric (yellow) tissue is worrisome.
- Oral temperature. The manatee's temperature may be assessed with a flexible oral probe placed as far back as possible in the mouth, between the cheek and the molars. Anything between 29 and 36 degrees Celsius is considered normal. Don't ask about rectal temperature. All that fermentation in the gut makes this method extremely unreliable.
- Blood chemistry and hematology. Blood is drawn from a flipper and centrifuged for plasma and serum separation.
- Eye exam.
- Genetic analysis using blood sampling.
- Collection of urine and feces.
- Pregnancy test for mature, nonlactating females by testing hormone levels.
- Capture stress levels.
- Examination of epiphytes (organisms like barnacles making their home on manatees).
- Trace element contaminant analysis in manatee tissues, which are then compared to levels in the local environment.
- Genetic studies to compare the Florida manatee with its West Indian cousin.

If not already present, the manatee is also fitted with two passive integrated transponder (PIT) tags—just a fancy name for a microchip, the same kind I hope you use for your dog. They are about the size of a grain of rice and inserted right below the skin. So far, researchers have conducted tests like this on hundreds of manatees, many in the waters of Crystal River, Florida. The information they gather is vital if we are to be successful in helping manatees achieve a stable thriving population.

A manatee tagging device includes a padded belt, a flexible tether, and a floating radio tag. Researchers tie the belt around the peduncle with a buckle and nylon webbing for a "custom fit." Juvenile and smaller manatees are fitted with a weaker belt that can easily break during a growth spurt. The buckle attaches to a four- or five-foot-long tether. It is designed so that when manatees are feeding at their typical six-foot depth in coastal waters, the floating tag transmits information from above the surface. The tether is specially designed to avoid entanglement; however, just in case something goes awry, a weak link is built into its base so the manatee can easily break free if caught. Each device is equipped with an ultrasonic beacon belt to facilitate field tracking via sonic receiver and hydrophone. Often a small temperature logger is attached to the base of the tether to gather information on the water temperatures.

The floating tag has three components: a GPS unit, a satellite transmitter, and a VHF transmitter. Each tag transmits a unique VHF frequency. One weakness of this system is that VHF signals don't transmit though salt water, where manatees spend a good portion of their time. So if the tag is pulled off underwater when the manatee is traveling or bottom resting in deep water, the manatee will escape monitoring. However, if scientists are within a few hundred yards of where the manatee fled, they can locate it using the ultrasonic beacon in the belt.

The GPS unit functions like the GPS in your car or cell phone. It can be programmed to "acquire" a location at any time interval and store the information in its memory; for example, a fifteen-minute GPS fixed interval can provide up to ninety-six locations per day for up to six months. The satellite-linked transmitter sends these GPS locations—along with data on tag activity, temperature, and diving behavior—to orbiting satellites through the Argos satellite system, a low earth orbit collection dedicated to studying and protecting our planet's environment. Manatee researchers download the data through a website, permitting remote monitoring of individual manatees in nearly real time! For visual identification, each float has a set of unique colored band combinations.

It's all very exciting, of course, except for the luckless manatees who have to endure the indignity of being tailed (in both senses of the word) in this fashion. Still, researchers have taken every precaution to make sure manatees can swim, play, mate, and rear their young normally while tagged. It's expensive, though, with a tag costing about $4,500. However, it's all for the good of science and presumably for the manatees as well. It is also temporary. At the end of each study, the belts, which are preprogrammed, automatically drop off the manatee at the assigned date and hour. If, for some odd reason, there's a failure in this department, a researcher will quietly approach the manatee and release it with a custom-made tool mounted on a pole. And if the manatee refuses to be approached, the hardware in his gear will corrode in the salt water and drop off after a while anyway.

Another less invasive (and less expensive) way to detect and track elusive manatees was announced in 2018 by U.S. Geological Survey (USGS) scientists, although work had begun five years earlier. Researchers figured out a way to extract manatee genetic material from their habitat using water samples collected in the field. The method, sensibly enough, is called environmental DNA detection, and it's the best way to track rare, elusive, and hard-to-find species. Hopefully, their efforts will eventually help restore manatees to their former glory in places like Brazil and West Africa. In any case, it works like this: Dr. Margaret Hunter of the USGS and her team isolated a unique DNA segment that is found in residues of the manatee body. We are talking about things like skin cells, saliva, and even exhaled water vapor! The team created a genetic marker to target the segment. The method works with all three manatee species; it also works in both fresh and salt water.

The test can be thwarted to some extent if there is a lot of tannins or other organic matter in the water. The biggest problem with the test is that it can't tell researchers how many animals are out there. Maybe just one, maybe forty-three. Also, conducting the test itself is a bit tricky. Still, it's a start and a great help in discovering if a particular area has been used by manatees, even if none is currently present. One suspects similar techniques will soon be applied to Yetis, Bigfoot, the Loch Ness monster, the Jersey Devil, and the Florida Skunk Ape.

At any rate, researchers have discovered that manatees are individualistic about their migratory patterns. Manatee migration patterns fall into several groups. The marathoners are officially classed as "long-distance migrants," making annual round trips of between seven hundred and more than a thousand miles per season; one exceptional male individual clocked almost three thousand miles annually. At the other end of the scale are the homebodies, who generally stay within fifty miles of their favorite spots. Those in between are classed as short-distance migrants and medium-distance migrants.

In general, manatee stay within their assigned migratory class. Each manatee finds its rhythm and pretty much sticks with it. In other words, homebodies do not tend to become long-distance migrants and vice versa.

The most famous manatee long-distance migrant is Chessie, named after the Chesapeake Bay, where he has been visiting since July 1994 (at least). Even after the water started to chill, Chessie seemed disinclined to return to Florida

Recently a manatee first identified in Crystal River in December 1979 and seen subsequently in other Florida rivers in 2005 and 2006 was spotted at a power plant in Cuba. Several other manatees and a calf were also observed. This behavior is typical of Florida, not Cuban manatees (who live in a more equable climate). Many found it surprising to see a manatee navigate such a large stretch of deep open water rather than moving close to shorelines. Some scientists believe that this phenomenon might be evidence that the waters of the Gulf of Mexico and the Florida Strait might be bridging rather than dividing the two populations. No one knows for sure what is going on, but dwindling natural habitat is a major contender.

and eventually had to be captured and rescued. He recuperated for a while at the National Aquarium in Baltimore. Then the Coast Guard flew him back home, and he was tagged and released. The next year, Chessie was on the move again. This time he stopped only briefly at the Chesapeake Bay, opting for Point Judith, Rhode Island, as his final destination. (This time, to everyone's relief, he went home on his own.) In June 1996, he headed north yet again, but lost his transmitter in Beaufort, North Carolina. (That's pronounced BO-fort. The Beaufort in South Carolina is pronounced BU-ford. But I suppose that's beside the point.) In August he was seen in the Great Bridge Locks in Virginia. Ten years passed before there was another sighting: this time in Calvert County, Maryland. Ten more years passed, and no one knew what had become of this intrepid traveler.

Then on February 5, 2021, the Florida Fish and Wildlife Conservation Commission rescued an emaciated manatee swimming sideways in the Lake Worth Lagoon near Riviera Beach, Florida. It was Chessie, struggling with buoyancy problems and generally awful body conditions. These are the same symptoms that starving manatees everywhere were exhibiting during this terrible year. Chessie's prognosis was poor. However, the veterinarians at SeaWorld worked their magic and on May 11, 2021, Chessie was deemed well enough to return to the wild. He was released at Anchorage Park in Palm Beach, and once again fitted with a tracking device. You guessed it: the satellite tag stopped transmitting in June, and researchers guessed it had been damaged by a boat or an alligator. Apparently, although alligators mostly leave manatees themselves alone, they have a sneaking fondness for biting off satellite tags. No one knew, however, what had happened to Chessie. Again. But lo and behold! On January 25, 2022, the Clearwater Aquarium deployed a hydrophone that detected a second (still operative) tracking device on the world-famous manatee. Chessie was taking his ease in the discharge from a warm-water power plant in Fort Lauderdale. Scientists scurried over there and quickly attached a new satellite tag. Now anyone who cares to can track him again. For a while at least. You can follow his movements yourself at https://mission.cmaquarium.org/news/manatee-tracking-chessie/.

In 2021, scientists from Dauphin Sea Island Lab in Alabama, the Department of Marine Sciences at the University of Southern Alabama, and the Clearwater Aquarium Institute in Clearwater, Florida, reported that manatees used "partial migration" to shift their geographic ranges to novel, more environmentally favorable regions (mainly to adapt to climate change). The subjects of the study were tagged manatees monitored by the ARGOS satellite system as well as by visual observation.

Partial migration simply means that only part of the population migrates and is in fact the most common migratory tactic of all migrating animals. With partial migration, some individuals switch between being residents and being migrators. Affecting the decision whether to migrate at all, when, or how far are a variety of factors including local temperature, quality of seagrass and other food, and competition. Observers have documented manatees in Mobile Bay, Alabama, since the early 1900s, but their numbers seem to be increasing, probably because the Gulf is heating up. Partial migration turns out to be a great tool in helping manatees cope with climate change. However, it has its disadvantages, especially for managing this endangered species.

We don't know how each animal "decides" to arrange its summer holiday. Scientists could find absolutely no correlation between the distance a manatee travels and its age, sex, size, or female reproductive state. It was noted that manatees traveled from one point to another rather quickly. Unlike what you might expect, they do not spend a lot of time drifting aimlessly around or socializing en route. They know where they are going and make haste to get there. Only a few areas are apparently designated as approved stopovers, places where there is access to fresh water and seagrass. (Manatees in the Indian River Lagoon show a strong preference for using the dredged-out channel of the Intracoastal Waterway.)

In the fall, when the manatees are in a major rush to get to warmer waters, about half the manatees do not stop at all. In the spring, about two-thirds of them take advantage of a rest. Calves travel with their mothers, of course, at least until they are weaned. At that point, they make their own decisions and choose their own path in life.

Some manatees are calendar types who seem to head for warmer waters on the same date every year (usually in November, no matter how warm it is) whereas others wait until a chill sets in and water temperatures fall below 68 degrees before heading south. More stubborn beasts wait even longer, until the temperatures reach a bitter 59 degrees. Once again, manatees stick to their own individual plans—those leaving at 68 degrees one year will continue to do so. And again, there is no difference in regard to sex, size, age, or maternal status. They are equally likely to move by night as day (the lack of a pineal gland apparently gives them this freedom). Some travel alone; others prefer company and move in small groups. They cover fifteen to twenty-two miles per day while on the march. When manatees reach their summer quarters, however, males do move around somewhat more than females, probably for obvious reasons.

The researchers used GPS data obtained from tagged critters who had migrated from between the northern Gulf of Mexico (usually Mobile Bay) and peninsular Florida (usually Crystal River). Most of the manatees seemed to prefer their northern Gulf residence until cold weather set in. The migration period ran between 10 and 133 days. (Those animals starting later understandably moved more quickly to avoid the cold and often skipped stopover points.)

SOS

Saving Our Sea Cows

Governments and individuals can work together to improve the lot of our sirenian cousins. Saving the sea cows will take money and dedication. Efforts can be divided into three main piles: rescue and rehabilitation, provisional feeding, and most critical habitat restoration. The Florida state legislature did provide $8 million for this purpose (a skimpy sum in my opinion) with the intent to "restore manatee access to springs" but the legislation has so many limitations, both in regard to time frame and content, it's difficult to see how much can be done. Note that many measures help manatees simply by improving the conditions of their habitat.

Here are some things that can be done. Some are a lot easier than others.

THINGS YOU CAN DO AS AN INDIVIDUAL

Educate both children and adults. The critical step is to create an informed public. Science has the answers, but unless the public is willing to implement necessary changes in legislation and to make personal lifestyle changes, it will all come to nothing. Only when everyone "gets" that an unhealthy environment is bad for everyone will they be willing to make the changes needed. Florida Fish and Wildlife Conservation (FWC) Commission, Save the Manatee Club, Treasure Coast Manatee Foundation, environmental centers, schools, and other organizations offer manatee-centered activities, lectures, educational materials, summer camps, and courses centered on manatees.

Report distressed, sick, injured, or dead manatees at 1-888-404-FWCC (3922) or use VHF channel 16 on your marine radio. You can also download the free FWC Reporter App on your smartphone or tablet.

Obey manatee zone speed limits when boating. They should also learn to recognize the characteristic lily-pad-shaped patterns in the water left by a manatee paddle.

Purchase Save the Manatee License Plates. Only if you live in Florida, though, right? The fee goes directly to the Save the Manatee Trust Fund, a major source of funding for the state's manatee research, rescue/rehabilitation, and conservation activities (https://myfwc.com/research/manatee/trust-fund/license-plate/).

Participate in local shoreline, beach, park, or roadside cleanup. Even if you are alone, take along a plastic bag and pick up litter. Dispose of it properly, of course.

Help monitor red tide as a citizen scientist. The Florida Fish and Wildlife Conservation Commission's Fish and Wildlife Research Institute's (FWRI) Red Tide Offshore Monitoring Program is looking for volunteers from Florida's coastal counties to collect water samples. Volunteers collect water samples at least once a month from bridges and docks alongshore or from locations at least one mile offshore. FWRI pays for supplies and shipping costs (https://myfwc.com/research/redtide/monitoring/current/coop/).

Join Save the Manatee Club's Manatee sighting network. If you live along a river, estuary, canal, or coastal area in Florida, you can help provide valuable information to researchers who are tracking manatees. When you spot a manatee, just fill out their online form or download a form to email, fax, or mail (www.savethemanatee.org/).

Plant native species for your yard and garden. Native plants do not need watering or fertilizer. That's why they are native. They provide host plants for butterflies. (Butterflies turn out to be very picky. Most of them feed on nectar from many plants but lay their eggs on only one.) They stabilize the soil around waterways. Turf should comprise, at most, only 20 percent of the lawn. Even that's a lot. People who plant native plants and ground covers instead of St. Augustine grass and other abominations are saving manatees.

Take advantage of (and press for more) state tax incentives for consumers to purchase electric vehicles and solar power for homes and business. All-electric and plug-in hybrid vehicles bought new in or after 2010 may be eligible for a $7,500 federal income tax credit. Check the Clean Energy Act for America for more information. State and municipal tax breaks may also be available. Florida's electric vehicle (EV) incentive program offers up to $300 in rebates to those who purchase or lease an EV. In addition, the Jacksonville Electric Authority offers up to $7,500 in tax credits.

Fight climate change. Do it for yourself, if not for the manatees. It impacts everyone.

Protect a pond. If you have a pond on your property, plant trees around the perimeter to help filter the water and lower the water table. Many Florida homes are encircled or partially encircled by swales. Please do not fill these in or plant a bunch of stuff in them. Keep them clear of grass clippings and trash. Any reduction in the ability of swales to do their job hurts everyone. If you use a blower on your driveway, you are required to blow the clippings onto your yard—not the swales or road. Direct rain gutters away from paved surfaces. Standard concrete is not helpful. Brick, porous concrete, or gravel is a much better choice for improving the environment. If your driveway is littered with leaves or clippings, it's much better to sweep it off rather than using a hose and getting all that oil into the swales and eventually the stormwater system.

Fish and aquaculture responsibly. Overfishing can destroy critical links in the food web. Anglers can also snare manatees (accidently but harmfully). Anglers need to be particularly careful of their lines, checking frequently for fraying. Monofilament lines should be disposed of properly. Braided lines should be cut into short segments and placed in a lidded trash can. Hooks should be clipped when you are done with them. It's not just manatees, but dolphins, turtles, and even dogs that can run afoul of them.

Fish farming, unless very carefully done, often leads to pumping more nutrients into the system. In the past, irresponsible fish farming has cleared critical mangrove forests to make room for shrimp and fishponds.

Support Save the Manatee Club. This organization is a prime advocacy group. Founded by former Florida governor Bob Graham and Jimmy Buffett, the organization runs an adopt-a-manatee program. Rumor has it that one would-be adopter was disgruntled to discover that a real live manatee would not be delivered to his home on a flatbed trunk after he'd adopted it, so let me be clear that this is a symbolic adoption only. They also have items to purchase through their website. The site also provides ways to contact decision makers to let them know how important the issue is to you.

THINGS ORGANIZATIONS ARE DOING

Support the Fish and Wildlife Foundation of Florida. The foundation supports many projects that protect and restore Florida's freshwater springs, essential habitats for Florida manatees. The Marine Mammal Fund is an important part of this endeavor (https://wildlifeflorida.org/).

NOAA's Marine Mammal Unusual Mortality Event Contingency Fund. The fund helps the Marine Mammal Health and Stranding Response Program respond to marine mammal unusual mortality events.

Join Save the Manatee Club's Manatee sighting network. If you live along a river, estuary, canal, or coastal area in Florida, you can help provide valuable information to researchers who are tracking manatees. When you spot a manatee, just fill out their online form or download a form to email, fax, or mail (www.savethemanatee.org/).

Support the Nature Conservancy's efforts. In partnership with the state, the conservancy is working to remove excessive sediment, restore natural creek depths, and improve the banks to reduce erosion and sedimentation in Warm Mineral Springs and Salt Creek for the one hundred Florida manatees that find refuge there during cold spells (www.nature.org/en-us/).

Convert and protect what little remains of natural lands rather than destroying wetlands for interstates, interchanges, and housing developments. (Florida, for all intents and purposes, is already "full.") Organizations like the Indian River Land Trust buy environmentally sensitive properties to maintain in a natural state (www.irlt.org/).

THINGS GOVERNMENT SHOULD BE DOING

End the dangerous practice of dumping human "biosoil" (read "poop") on lands. Instead, we need to build effective water-treatment facilities in which liquids can be cleansed to potable levels and solids can be used for fertilizer and electricity. In Florida, fertilizers with phosphorus are especially dangerous. Florida has enough phosphorus in the ground already without dumping more of the stuff. Currently we release 2.5 million pounds of nitrogen and phosphorus into the estuary every year from septic tanks, lawns and farms (www.fisheries.noaa.gov/national/marine-life-distress/marine-mammal-unusual-mortality-event-contingency-fund).

Improve stormwater treatments and swales. During storms, runoff from buildings, parking lots, and sidewalks flows quickly to the lowest level it can, bringing with it chemicals, oil, silt, and trash. This material needs to be cleaned before it enters the estuaries and ocean. Basically, there are two ways to handle this runoff: retention and detention systems. Retention systems collect runoff and let it seep through the ground. These systems include swales, or grassy ditches that help filter the sediments as they enter the soil. Detention systems are just ponds specifically designed to allow the sediments to be absorbed and "settle" as they are slowly released into the ground. They should include a lot of shoreline vegetation to help filter the runoff. Local governments can obtain low interest loans for stormwater infrastructure via the Clean Water State Revolving Fund. Help is also available through the Clean Water Act, section 319 (h). And the Total Maximum Daily Load Water Quality Grant (I'm not happy with this massive noun cluster, but there you have it). Florida also receives about $6 million annually from the Environmental Protection Agency for high-priority projects restoring water quality to impaired springs, rivers, and estuaries.

Restore the Great Florida Riverway. The Ocklawaha River was dammed in 1968. The dam flooded more than 7,500 acres of forested wetlands and twenty springs. If the dam were breached, we could reestablish access to essential habitat for manatees, bring back migratory fish, connect three river ecosystems, and restore a lost riverway for anglers and paddlers.

Replace septic tanks with modern, well-maintained sewer systems. This can be done. Around 2012 the city of Stewart began replacing its remaining 2,200 septic tanks. The city is now completely sewered. Other municipalities can do the same. This is especially critical in places where septic tanks are densely clustered and close to a river, spring, or estuary. State funds from environmental agencies are available to help. Granted, this is a difficult task in settled communities where streets have to be dug up. But the process is critical for the health of the lagoon. Temporary disruption is surely worth avoiding further die-offs of seagrass, manatees, pelicans, fish, and dolphins. And to get rid of the algae superblooms. Where sewer is not yet available, require advanced-technology septic systems.

Support efforts to reduce the unconscionable explosion of plastic in our environment. Microplastics have recently been found in human lungs, even in the deepest tissues. Almost all plastic comes from fossil fuels, so plastic is a problem at *all* stages in its life cycle, not just in the final product.

Eliminate chemicals like glyphosate, atrazine, and other toxic chemicals used to "treat" invasives, which can be mechanically removed instead (and recycled). This will improve human health as well, as it is strongly suspected glyphosate is a human carcinogen. And yet, a 2017 study by Paul Mills, professor of family medicine and public health at the University of California, San Diego, in a peer-reviewed study in *JAMA*, found that between 1994 and 2016, the percentage of people who tested positive for glyphosate rose 500 percent. And the level of the chemical spiked by more than *1,000 percent*. Why dump it in the Indian River Lagoon? Some local governments are still using this stuff.

Restore native habitats, especially mangroves and salt marshes. A healthy lagoon depends on healthy lands surrounding it. Red mangroves (*Rhizophora mangle*) in particular play a critical role for many species, including arthropods, mollusks, marine worms, sponges (fourteen species), tunicates (thirty-nine species), hydroids, and bryozoans ("moss animals"). Wading birds, moon jellies, comb jellies, and sargassum weeds also can be observed passing through. Manatees use them as resting spots and places to give birth and nurse their young.

Reduce erosion and bank collapse at primary refuge sites. Here's a success story. At the fifty-seven-acre Three Sisters Springs, the annual influx of tourists is extremely "challenging," creating shoreline erosion and siltation in Florida's second-largest spring system. Interestingly, at one time the area was cleared to prepare for a three-hundred-unit waterfront development. But then something happened. A young manatee was injured in a boat collision, and the investors, who were on hand, helped with the rescue. That experience changed their minds, and the project was abandoned. Unfortunately, just a narrow band of native vegetation around the springs was left. The land was put up for sale and the Friends of Crystal River National Wildlife Refuge Complex worked with the Florida Communities Trust to buy it in 2010 for $10.5 million. (The City of Crystal River and Southwest Florida Water Management District share ownership; the U.S. Fish and Wildlife Service manages the property as part of the Crystal River National Wildlife Refuge.) Conservation managers noted that the springs' banks were weakening. Trees had fallen into the water, and hungry manatees were chewing exposed roots, creating even more erosion. Sediment was accumulating over the spring vents. Water quality degraded. A restoration plan was developed using soil fill made of Envirolok, a nonwoven fabric that tree roots easily grow through. Over time, the fabric decays. As the tree roots lock together, the soil is stabilized. Additional support was provided using limestone boulders (limestone is native to Florida) under a firm foundation of pea gravel. Native trees and other vegetation were planted. The result looks like part of a natural landscape, not a concrete seawall.

Fully implement the Blue-Green Algae Task Force's recommendations. The task force, an advisory body to the governor, is particularly concerned about Lake Okeechobee, Caloosahatchee Estuary, and St. Lucie River and Estuary areas. It recognizes an "urgent" need to manage flows to reduce the amount of damaging freshwater influxes in the estuaries, especially the Indian River Lagoon. They also have specific recommendations for better management of agricultural lands, human waste, and stormwater treatment systems.

Stop Lake Okeechobee discharges into the Indian River Lagoon via the St. Lucie River. Though the Blue Green Algae Task Force has some ideas about the need to reduce the flow (which is not natural, but artificially created), other organizations press for a stronger solution. And the same practices that are dumping unwanted nutrients in the estuaries on the East and West Coasts are also starving Florida Bay of the natural freshwater it needs. Currently, the lake is diked to form a reservoir and is regulated by control gates at several outlets. The Army Corps of Engineers has a lot to say about all this, and its interests do not necessarily coincide with those of the manatees—or the environment. Its main mission is concern for human safety—hence the concern for keeping Lake O from flooding. In the natural way of things, Lake Okeechobee overflowed its banks in the wet season, sending sheets of fresh (and unpolluted) waters south to the Everglades. However, the 1928 hurricane, which killed many people living in the area, initiated a series of construction projects to "control" the lake. In truth, the real lesson is that this natural area isn't really suitable for human habitation. Anyway, over seven years, the Army Corps of Engineers built a series of levees, locks, and culverts. The lake, which used to boast of some the greatest fishing on earth, is now polluted from the cattle and sugar industry. And the Army Corps of Engineers is now sending the polluted waters east and west rather than south.

During the dry season, outflows are reduced to slow the recession of the lake and reduce—but not eliminate—the dangerous release of fresh water into the brackish lagoon. For example, in April 2022, the releases to the Caloosahatchee Estuary will target a pulse release at a seven-day average of 1,500 cubic feet per second from the W. P. Franklin Lock and Dam (S-79). This is a gradual reduction from the level of 2,000 cubic feet per second, which had been in place since November, and the 1,800 targeted pulse release that was initiated on April 2. That is still a lot of bad water. Several lawmakers and a lot of the public want to stop Okeechobee releases for good, in the belief that stinking, slimy algae or sludge-colored waters isn't the best look for the tourist-dependent region. The only solution people can seem to come up with is to build more infrastructure (holding tanks) around the lake. Sadly, this will take too long. The unfortunate fact is that nature intended for Lake Okeechobee to perform like this.

Legislate that water from the Florida aquifer should be used for drinking, cooking, and bathing only, not for watering golf courses. An aquifer is a collection of water-bearing sedimentary rocks. In Florida, we have two types: siliciclastics (sands, silts, clays) and carbonates (limestone and dolostone). They may look solid, but they contain empty places that can hold water. They are both porous (with holes) and permeable made so that the holes connect with each other and let water flow through. The Floridan aquifer system (FAS), which underlies all of Florida, is an 82,000-square-mile reservoir that holds billions of gallons of fresh water. Some of this water may be 26,000 years old. It's the primary source of potable groundwater for much of the state. (In the extreme western panhandle, the aquifer is a bit too deep and in south Florida a bit too salty for this use.) Residents of Florida use about 100 to 150 gallons of water every day. Indoors, about 24 percent of a household's water goes to flushing toilets. And another 20 percent is used to keep people clean. The rest is used to run water—laundry, dishes, and so on. But half of all the water taken from the public supply (which mostly come from the aquifer) ends up watering private lawns—some 900 million gallons a day. Overextraction, sea-level rise, and an increasing saltwater intrusion are all straining our aquifer to the limit.

Support the Seagrass Nursery Network in promoting outplanting and preserving genetic diversity. Data collected by Dennis Hanisak of Harbor Branch Oceanographic

Institute (Florida Atlantic University) shows that patches of seagrasses at depths of one to three feet can hang in there for up to twenty-four years. Perhaps seagrass at this depth zone holds the key to recovery—which still may take as long as seventeen years. This dire situation led him and his colleagues to work on better land-based ways to accelerate seagrass recovery, planting the grass in large tanks and then transplanting it to the lagoon. (When you plant it directly in the lagoon, it tends to die.) The Florida Fish and Wildlife Conservation Commission is funding the expansion of the seagrass nursery. Florida Power and Light is supplying the money to operate the nursery for at least three years. By enriching the sediment the experimental seagrass grows in, the researchers hope to be able to grow more seagrass faster than ever.

Support the Indian River Lagoon Clam and Seagrass Restoration Initiative, which aims to restore twelve million native clams as well as seagrass. The Indian River Lagoon Clam Restoration Initiative, developed by the Whitney Laboratory (University of Florida) is now in its third year. In 2019, adult *Mercenaria mercenaria* clams were collected from Mosquito Lagoon and spawned. These were tough "superclams," which had survived the brown tide and hypoxic event of 2012 and subsequent harmful algal blooms. Dr. Todd Osborne considered these clams to have genetically superior survival skills. Brevard Zoo is in partnership with the project. This will establish a new clam gardener program that will create one hundred clam grow-out sites within Brevard County that will be monitored by citizen scientists (who could be you).

Cap the lagoon muck with sand to create suitable seagrass habitat. The Indian River Lagoon also has a muck problem. Decades of organic matter flowing into the lagoon from human development has settled to the bottom as muck, a gooey substance that leaches nutrients into the water column. What goes into the lagoon stays in the lagoon.

Although dredging the muck has been the go-to plan for decades (aside from doing absolutely nothing, which also has its adherents), capping the muck may be a better solution. Dredging usually goes too deep below the "photic" zone, and seagrass wouldn't have enough light to survive. Other benthic systems may suffer similarly. Although not historically used in Florida, capping is a well-known procedure in other places. It's been demonstrated through research that this method will significantly reduce nitrogen/phosphorus flux. It will also avoid a perennial problem with muck dredging—which is, what do we do with the dredged muck? It will also create a shallower environment better for habitat development. A similar plan would be subaqueous placement/capping and habitat restoration.

Epilogue

"They sure are homely," remarked the woman next to me, leaning over the wooden bridge railing as far as she could while clicking her cell phone, trying to snap photos of the large spindle shapes gliding below.

"I think they're just beautiful," I countered.

"They have faces like tushes," she pointed out, accurately but unkindly.

Suddenly a stiff-whiskered head emerged partly from the smooth surface of the water. The creature it belonged to snorted explosively, expelling a huge lungful of air into the early morning half-light. Nearby, a fart bubbled softly up. A fluke smacked and then one flipper waved awkwardly in the air as the animal slowly rolled over in front of us. It swam upside down for a while and then sank out of sight, leaving nothing but a "footpad" of water. I tugged lightly at the cord of my hydrophone, designed to capture the squeaks and chirps emitted below the surface by the massive animals, which dangled in the water. "I don't know," I said. "I think they're really beautiful."

The woman snorted, sounding a bit like a manatee herself. "I think that's manatee poop," she announced as a piece of something greenish and brownish floated by.

"Yeah," I agreed. "It is."

Manatees are a test case. If we can save these large, extraordinary, magical creatures, maybe we can save ourselves.

The manatee is our state marine mammal (even though it is not strictly marine). We have a state saltwater mammal, too—the dolphin—a fact that creates immediate confusion. So far as I know, there is no difference between a marine and a saltwater mammal. It seems to be a grab to stake claim to as many "state animals" as possible.

For the record, the Florida state animal is the Florida panther, which is critically endangered. (Until 1958 you could actually hunt them.)

The state reptile is of course the alligator. Although other states also host the occasional alligator, Florida is the only one that hosts them in every county.

We share our state bird, the mockingbird, with a host of other states. (We could have selected the supremely endangered grasshopper sparrow, which could use some good publicity. (We also might have picked the more handsome, charming, endemic, and brilliantly friendly scrub jay, but no. . . .) There's a political reason behind the snubbing of the scrub jay, which involves citrus growers and the National Rifle Association, but I can't go into all that now.

Our state butterfly is the handsome zebra longwing, an excellent choice.

The state saltwater fish is the sailfish (hardly unique to Florida, that one).

The state freshwater fish is the largemouth bass. They live in places other than Florida but for some reason get really *big here.*

The state shell is the horse conch, the exoskeleton of a very large and predatory sea snail. Perfect.

I suppose we could, just for the heck of it, proceed to the state flower: the orange blossom. Oranges aren't native, but they are delicious, fragrant, beautiful, and grow here.

Our state beverage is of course, orange juice, despite anything you may hear about Margaritaville. (We might get to Jimmy Buffett later. There's a strong manatee connection.)

The state wildflower is the coreopsis, a pretty but uninspired choice.

Our state tree is the cabbage palm, which grows everywhere around here.

Our state stone is (wait for it): coral. Coral is an animal.

Our state gemstone is the moonstone. No, there is no moonstone in Florida. There's no moonstone on the moon, either, but this gem was chosen because astronauts left for the moon from Florida.

We have a state soil too, which is not actually sand, as you might think, but Myakka soil, which is unique to Florida and useful for agriculture. We have a few million acres of the stuff.

Our state motto is "In God we trust." I do not know why.

We now have a state dessert. It is strawberry shortcake with natural Florida dairy topping. This is in honor of Florida strawberry farmers who produce 75 percent of the winter strawberry crop for the United States. I don't know what happened to key lime pie. I just don't.

We have had more than one state song. The original one (1913) was "Florida, My Florida." Then someone decided they liked Stephen Foster's "Way Down upon the Suwanee River" ("Old Folks at Home"). Foster never visited Florida, but he did like the sound of the name Suwanee. It fit the music. However, after a while, people finally woke up to how racist the song was and changed the lyrics.

Not satisfied with a revised state song, we decided to add a state anthem*: "Florida Where the Seagrass Meets the Sky," a work that fulfills the promise of its name, containing such immortal lines as, "Sitting proud in the ocean like a sentinel true / Always shielding your own, yet giving welcome" and "The orange blossoms' sweet perfume and fireworks fill the air / And cultures rich our native people share." Actually, the indigenous people who live here now were not in fact originally from Florida. Those people, the Ais, were extirpated by the Spanish and others. We have a state play about the whole conquest, called* Cross and Sword. *Apparently, the costumes are interesting.*

We don't seem to have a state insect. Officially, that is. Several candidates for the role have presented themselves over the years, including palmetto bugs, lovebugs, mosquitoes, and fire ants. All worthy contenders.

To report an injured manatee, call 888-404-3922

Index

Page references for figures are italicized.